#1 *NEW YORK TIMES* BESTSELLING AUTHOR

MIKE EVANS

LIGHTS
IN THE
DARKNESS

HEROES *of the* HOLOCAUST

TimeWorthy
BOOKS

P.O. Box 30000, Phoenix, AZ 85046

Lights in the Darkness is dedicated to
Ambassador Rami Levi
who served as Israel's Special Emissary to the
Evangelical Community and who did so much to
encourage the relationship between Israel and
the Friends of Zion. On a personal note, Rami is
my dearest friend and my senior advisor.

PREFACE

"Character is doing the right thing even when it costs
more than you want to pay. . . . Character is not a fancy
coat we put on for show, it's who we really are."

—MICHAEL JOSEPHSON[1]

In Belgium during the Holocaust, a complex system was established to rescue Jewish children. It was composed of both Jews and Gentiles working together to see that the youngest in society were not faced with the horrors of the Holocaust.

The decision to send children into hiding was a gut-wrenching one that many parents were forced to make. Families were compelled to come to terms with the probability that parents would never see their offspring again. Children, if they survived, would grow up not knowing their birth parents. Practicality dictated that it was easier to conceal one child than to take in an entire family. There were times when a parent, usually the mother, could accompany a child. The majority of the men had been conscripted into labor camps by the time such a decision had to be made. Often it was a mother who had to come to terms with giving her child to a stranger or eventually seeing them herded into a gas chamber or executed in a pit already filled with bodies.

Christians across Europe stepped forward and reached out with willing arms to receive a child who needed sanctuary, most often at the risk of losing their own lives. I am moved by the poetry of Hannah Senesh, arrested for "humanitarian acts" for trying to help Jews reach safety. She wrote from inside Ravensbruck: "I gambled on what mattered most, the dice were cast. I lost."[2]

As you will see in the pages of this book, we have much to learn from those ordinary people who stood for right and refused to succumb to the evil forces around them. Those "evil forces" were most often the *Schutzstaffel*, or SS, which included the dreaded Gestapo and the vicious and pitiless guards who populated the internment and death camps. Recruited to serve Hitler as his personal bodyguard, those selected were forced to prove their Aryan ancestry for more than 200 years. Author Susan Brophy Down wrote:

> SS officers were trained to turn a blind eye to human suffering. They were schooled in racial hatred as part of their training to carry out the

campaign to exterminate Europe's Jews and other minorities.[3]

While many during that time turned their backs and refused to see the conflagration of anti-Semitism that was roaring across Eastern Europe, people of character took extraordinary actions; miracles happened. People such as Miep and Jan Gies, Oskar Schindler, Irena Sendler, Chiune Sugihara, the ten Boom family, Raoul Wallenberg, and the populace of Le Chambon-sur-Lignon, France, made a difference in the lives of a multitude of Jewish people—survivors of the Holocaust due to the acts of many brave men and women.

In the words of Dr. Martin Luther King Jr.:

Darkness cannot drive out darkness: only light can do that.[4]

MIEP GIES

*"Look at how a single candle can both
defy and define the darkness."*

—ANNE FRANK

1

On January 29, 1991, President George H. W. Bush stepped to the podium in the House chamber of the United States Capitol Building to deliver the State of the Union Address. One phrase in particular captured the imagination of those listening. The president challenged the attendees and, indeed, all who heard when he opined:

> We have within our reach the promise of a renewed America. We can find meaning and reward by serving some purpose higher than ourselves—a shining purpose, *the illumination of a thousand points of light*. It is expressed by all who know the irresistible force of a child's hand, of a friend who stands by you and stays there—a volunteer's generous gesture, an idea

that is simply right. The problems before us may
be different, but the key to solving them remains
the same: it is the individual—the individual
who steps forward . . . we must step forward
and accept our responsibility to lead the world
away from the dark chaos of dictators, toward
the bright promise of a better day.[5] (Emphasis
mine.)

These same words could well have been conveyed to the
Dutch people—and indeed, all Europeans—in December
1941 when the Nazis began to draw the noose tighter on
Jews in Holland and the Dutch were forbidden to give succor to them. Yet there were many brave people who defied
those orders and provided aid to their Jewish friends and
neighbors; imminently notable names are among those who
risked their lives to save some, including that of Hermine
"Miep" Gies, the short-in-stature, tall-in-courage woman
who harbored Anne Frank and her family.

The Franks were a German-Jewish family who had
moved from their native Germany to the Netherlands to
escape Adolf Hitler's "Final Solution"—the annihilation of
the Jewish race. Anne, her parents, Otto and Edith, and
older sister, Margot, hid in rooms above her father's office

in an attempt to escape deportation to the German work camps. While there, she wrote her thoughts daily in a diary that would be published in 1947. Anne disguised the names of those in hiding and those who aided them in an attempt to protect their identities should the Nazis raid their secret place. Her diary was a powerful message of perseverance and courage during those dark days.

Miep and her husband, Jan, were two brave souls who felt that people mattered, and they were determined to make a difference even in the face of adversity. Miep soon realized that she could not stand idly by and see men and women destroyed simply because they were Jewish. And those of similar conviction —brave rescuers all—knew that a decision made in the blink of an eye could mean life or death for an innocent victim of rabid anti-Semitism, and for themselves. Many of those who acted on principle did so as a result of a caring, compassionate upbringing.

Hannah Senesh, herself a victim of the Holocaust, wrote:

> There are stars whose radiance is visible
> on Earth though they have long been extinct.
> There are people whose brilliance continues
> to light the world though they are no longer
> among the living.[6]

Leery of being labeled a hero by others, Miep wrote:

> I am not a hero. I stand at the end of the long,
> long line of good Dutch people who did what I
> did or more—much more—during those dark
> and terrible times years ago, but always like
> yesterday in the hearts of those of us who bear
> witness. Never a day goes by that I do not think
> of what happened then.
>
> More than twenty thousand Dutch people
> helped to hide Jews and others in need of hid-
> ing during those years. I willingly did what I
> could to help. My husband did as well. It was
> not enough.[7]

Miep, born in Vienna, was frequently ill as a child. In 1930, after a rather severe bout with tuberculosis and suffer- ing the debilitating effects of malnutrition, the eleven-year- old was sent to live with total strangers at Gaaspstraat 5 in Amsterdam. The Nieuwenhuise (aka Nieuwenburg) family and their five children opened their hearts and home to the sickly young girl.

Miep had been born into the Catholic working-class Santruschitz family in Austria on February 15, 1909, just short years before the launch of World War I. Following the privations caused by the fighting in Europe and the addition of a sister, Miep was slowly dwindling to nothing. Her sticklike legs barely supported her small frame, and the lack of proper nutrition left her susceptible to various ailments. As a means to save their daughter, her parents, in an act of incredible love and sacrifice, made arrangements for her to be sent to a foster family in the Netherlands in order to save her life.

One bitterly cold winter day, Miep's mother bundled her into whatever could be found to keep her warm and tied Miep's long hair back with a length of cotton fashioned into a large hair bow. Soon thereafter, her father took her hand and walked her to the Vienna train station. There he waited with her while she was examined by physicians. A lanyard with the names of her foster parents written on it was draped around her neck, and she boarded the huge, noisy train headed for she knew not where. As Miep settled into her seat, the train lurched forward and slowly moved away from the station. She and a large group of other terrified children soon began to realize that their parents were outside on the station platform and they were inside being borne away, not knowing what would become of them at the end of the journey.

Miep was so weak from the bout of tuberculosis and

malnourishment that the rocking motion of the train car soon lulled her to sleep. Sometime in the middle of the cold, dark night, a hand shook her awake and Miep struggled to focus on her surroundings. The sign outside the depot read: Leiden. The sleepy children were led from the train into a cavernous room where they were placed in chairs lined around the walls.

Suddenly, as if a horde of locusts had descended from the skies, a group of adults rushed into the room and began to clutch at the cards that swung from the necks of the boys and girls. Soon, a very solid and sturdy man walked up to Miep and reached for the card. He read the name printed on the tag and uttered a strange sound: *"Ja!"* (Dutch for "yes.") He had found the child whose nametag was a match. Gathering the little girl and her meager belongings, the two strangers to each other began the long trek to the Nieuwenhuise home outside Amsterdam. Miep struggled to keep up with her benefactor; the journey seemed to last forever.

Finally the two reached their destination and the man turned and led them into the hallway of a house. A woman, her face unremarkable but her eyes filled with compassion, took Miep by the hand and guided her to the kitchen, where she gave the child a cold glass of milk. Then again taking her hand, she led Miep up a flight of stairs to an attic room, which held twin beds. One bed was occupied by Catherina, a daughter of the house; the other, piled high with quilts, was for their new foster child. Miep's layers of clothing were quickly removed; she was slipped into a nightdress and tucked beneath the warm bedding. Trepidation was soon replaced by welcome sleep. The sickly young girl had found a welcoming and loving family—one she would never again leave. She was home.

A three-month stay turned into six months, and then nine. She was incorporated into the new household, learned Dutch, and began school, where she soon excelled. Despite their modest income, the family shared with her everything they had. The love and compassion she received impressed Miep profoundly and she later decided to make Holland her permanent home. Miep was deeply influenced by the values of her foster family. She would never forget the kindness shown by her hosts:

> Despite the language problem, all children were kind to me. Kindness, in my depleted condition, was very important to me. It was medicine as much as the bread, the marmalade, the good Dutch milk and butter and cheese, the toasty temperature of the warm rooms.[8]

After two years living on the outskirts of Amsterdam, the family and Miep moved into an area of the city known as River Quarter, South Amsterdam. It was quite a change from country life to streetcars attached to overhead electric cables, boats plying the canals, outdoor shops filled with brightly colored tulips, theaters and concert venues. After Miep turned sixteen, the Nieuwenhuises took her back to Vienna to visit her parents. Her five-year absence made the reunion awkward. Miep discovered she could no longer be happy in Austria, a fact that her parents soon echoed. Sadly, they agreed that their little Hermine should return to Amsterdam with her foster family. Her one mistake, she would later discover, was in not having her passport changed to indicate that she was no longer an Austrian citizen, but a Dutch citizen. Miep subsequently visited her parents again in 1933. After that visit, she wrote:

> When I bade farewell to my mother, father, and sister in Austria, I did so with a clarity about my identity. I knew I would continue to write and send money regularly, that I would periodically visit them and bring my children to see them when that time came, but that Holland would be my home forever.[9]

Also in 1933, at the age of twenty-four, Miep met the man to whom her destiny would be forever tied—Otto Frank. A neighbor, Mrs. Blik, had supplied Miep with a referral for a temporary job in Mr. Frank's office. Soon after being hired, Miep discovered that Mr. Frank, a Jew, and his family had left Germany because of the rise in power and influence of Adolf Hitler. Although Otto had taken up employment in Amsterdam, his family was still in Aachen, Germany, but planned to join him.

After several months of working in Otto's office, Miep was offered permanent employment at Opekta. She learned one day that Otto had rented an apartment in the same South Amsterdam area as her adopted family where the Franks were to join their husband and father. Her first meeting with Anne Frank took place in the office where she sat with Anne while her mother and father took coffee. Miep remembered that encounter: "Watching Anne, I thought, 'Now, here's the kind of child I would like to have someday. Quiet, obedient, curious about everything.'"[10]

Little did Miep know that as the clouds settled over Germany and Hitler implemented his infamous Final Solution, Anne would look to her for safekeeping. Miep had a taste of the anti-Semitism that plagued the Jews when the lady she had replaced, Miss Heel, returned to the office and began to spout disdain for all the Jewish refugees who had fled Germany. Miep quickly silenced her vitriol, but the atmosphere in the office descended into one of taut detachment.

2

I n March 1938, the office staff of Opekta and Company gathered around Otto's radio to listen to the announcement that Hitler's troops had made a celebratory entrance into Vienna, the city where Hitler had spent his youth. Austrian writer Carl Zuckmayer penned a horrific description of the nights following the Nazis' invasion of the city.

> The underworld had opened its gates and let loose its lowest, vilest, most unclean spirits. The city changed into a nightmare painting of Hieronymus Bosch: evil spirits and half demons seemed to crawl out of the filth and from swampy holes in the earth. The air was filled with unceasing, yelling, wild, hysterical

screaming from male and female gullets that screeched for days and nights on end . . . . What was unleashed here was the revolt of envy, grudge, bitterness, blind and evil vindictiveness—and all other voices were condemned to silence . . . a blind fury of destruction and hatred was directed at everything that nature or spirit ennobled. It was the witch's Sabbath of the rabble and the burial of all human dignity.[11]

The radio announcement hardly conveyed the reality of the events that were, even then, taking place in Vienna— the debasement of the Jews, the robberies, the looting, the debauchery inflicted on men and women, young and old. Nazi swastikas were hoisted over government buildings throughout Austria. Shortly thereafter, Miep was asked to join a Nazi association of women and girls, an organization that had established chapters in the countries that had either been occupied by or were threatened by Hitler's invasion. When time came for Miep's yearly visit to police headquarters in Amsterdam to have her passport stamped and visa renewed, she was appalled at being directed to the German consulate. There, her Austrian passport was seized and she was handed a new passport stamped with a black swastika.

Wondering if it was the result of her refusal to join the club, Miep was stunned. Her lifeline to Amsterdam had been invalidated. She was ordered to leave the city within three months . . . unless she married a Dutch citizen.

Miep had met her future husband, Jan, while both were employed at a textile factory. Their friendship blossomed and flourished after she went to work for Otto Frank. Their courtship spanned several years before they were able even to become engaged. The couple spent quite some time trying to find rooms to let, but a shortage of living space due to an influx of refugees fleeing the advance of Hitler's troops hindered their search. Austria had fallen in 1938, Poland in 1939, and the Netherlands was targeted in 1940.

Miep knew she wanted to become Mrs. Gies, and while she and Jan were eager to marry, they lacked three things necessary to do so: a copy of Miep's birth certificate from Vienna, sufficient funds to have the wedding, and an apartment. Within the space of about three months, and with the help of a compassionate lady in the city hall in Vienna, Miep's uncle who had been charged with securing the paperwork had been successful: She had a copy of her birth certificate in hand. Meanwhile, Otto had helped secure rooms for them in the home of a Jewish lady whose husband had fled to England. The young couple had also been able to save the necessary fees for the wedding. As soon as Miep had her paperwork in order, she and Jan set a wedding date—July 16, 1941.

On July 17, Miep and Jan were honored with a wedding feast at the offices where she and Otto Frank worked. This welcome respite from the outside world was a distraction from the increasingly stringent measures enacted on Jews in the Netherlands by the invading Nazi army. Dutch Jews had been forbidden to visit local eating establishments, attend movies or plays, stay in hotels, utilize the library, or even picnic in local parks. Radios had to be surrendered to the local constabulary—in good working order. And it ultimately became a criminal act for Jews and Christians to fraternize.

Weekend afternoons were spent at the Frank home in an area of Amsterdam known as Merwedeplein, a district in the southern sector of the city. It was there the Frank family resided as their freedoms shrank day by day until they had to leave their beautiful home behind for "The Secret Annex" that had been prepared as their hiding place in Mr. Frank's office building.

These get-togethers had to be halted because of encroaching Nazi restrictions on Jews, and eventually Otto, fearing what the invaders might do to his employees, asked Jan to take over his post as office head of Pectacon. The name was changed to Gies and Company and duly registered with the public notary in Amsterdam. In a few short months, all Jews in the country would be forced to sew to their clothing the yellow Star of David with the word *Jood* in the center.

Joseph Koek, who was a Jewish boy during World War II, allows us a glimpse of life in the Netherlands after the German army crossed the border:

> After the Nazi invasion of May 5, 1940 everything changed. The fear didn't begin to come 'til later when I was not allowed to go to stores that were owned by some people. And then I had to start wearing the yellow star on my suit with the word Jew on it. And that curfew started to get earlier and earlier until the family could barely get out of the house.
>
> On August 18, 1942 our family received a letter ordering us to report to the train station to be transported to what they said was a work camp. Later as an adult [I] came to realize that my parents must have been laying plans to escape for a very long time unbeknownst to my sisters and me. Because the next day I'm leaving home with a resistance guide. He's a total

stranger but we talk as he takes me to the end of the street and as we turn we keep walking until we get to the home where we'll spend the next few years in hiding . . . .

We found out that our parents had been betrayed and arrested by the Gestapo. They were picked up and they were transported to the camp at Auschwitz where they were murdered.[12]

Soon after the wedding celebration, Otto Frank informed Miep that he and his family were also considering going into hiding. He asked her a life-changing question: "Miep, are you willing to take on the responsibility of taking care of us while we are in hiding?"[13] When she responded affirmatively, he added, "Miep, for those who help Jews, the punishment is harsh; imprisonment, perhaps . . . "[14] She cross-examined him no further, feeling that the less she knew, the less she could convey to others if questioned.

On July 5, 1942, Jan and Miep were shaken from their Sunday evening pursuits by the jarring ringing of the door-bell. With some apprehension because of the anxiety caused by German occupation Jan hurried to the door. Hermann van Daan (aka Hermann van Pels) stood on the steps.

He was an employee of Otto Frank's company, a German Jew and former butcher who specialized in herbs used in sausage production. When he and Miep had first met, he would have her accompany him on visits to his friend, the local butcher. She wondered why those trips, but in time she would understand. Hermann urged Jan and Miep to quickly accompany him to the Franks' home. Margot, the older daughter, had been instructed to report for duty at a "work camp" in Germany. As a result of the notification, the Frank family had decided to seek immediate concealment in an area of the plant known as the Secret Annex, or *Het Achterhuis*. Miep and Jan were needed to transport personal belongings. That night, the two made trip after trip to their new lodgings from the Frank home hauling belongings hidden beneath their outsized coats. There, the goods would remain until they could safely be taken to the Secret Annex. Finally, on a rainy Monday morning, Miep rode her bicycle to get Margot and transfer her to the hiding place. According to Miep:

> No sooner had I reached the front stoop than the door of the Franks' apartment opened and Margot emerged . . . . Mr. and Mrs. Frank looked at me . . . . I made an effort to be assuring. "Don't

worry. The rain is very heavy . . . ." Without a backward glance, Margot and I pushed our bicycles onto the street . . . . We pedaled evenly, not too fast, in order to appear like two everyday working girls on their way to work on a Monday morning . . . . There we were, a Christian and a Jew without the yellow star, riding on an illegal bike. [All Jews had been forced to turn their bikes in to the Nazis.] And at a time when the Jew was ordered to report for a forced-labor brigade about to leave for parts unknown in Hitler's Germany . . . . Suddenly, we had become two allies against the might of the German beast among us.[15]

Arriving at the office, Miep led Margot to the entrance of the secret hiding space. She then returned to her desk to await the arrival of Margot's parents and sister, Anne. The aura of bleakness surrounding family members when they arrived at the office was difficult for Miep, but she went right to work shepherding the family upstairs into the Secret Annex. There they remained for twenty-five months in what would become increasingly cramped quarters.

A week later, the Franks were reunited with another family of Jewish friends, Hermann and Auguste van Pels and their son Peter (Alfred van Daan), who was fifteen. The three new arrivals moved into the upper floor of the Secret Annex. November saw the appearance of yet another acquaintance, dentist Dr. Fritz Pfeffer (the Albert Dussel of Anne's diary. The name means "idiot" or "donkey" in German.) In 1938, fearing the onslaught of anti-Semitism in Germany and the Netherlands, Dr. Pfeffer had sent Werner, his son from a first marriage, to England to live with relatives. With his arrival, Margot moved into the bedroom with her parents, and Anne was left to share a room with the older Dr. Pfeffer. She was not pleased with what she saw as his persnickety ways:

As if I don't hear "shh, shh" enough during the day because I'm always making "too much" noise, my dear roommate has come up with the idea of saying "shh, shh" to me all night too. According to him, I shouldn't even turn over. I refuse to take any notice of him, and the next time he shushes me, I'm going to shush him right back. He gets more exasperating and egotistical as the days go by. Except for the first week, I haven't seen even one of the cookies he so generously promised me. He's particularly infuriating on Sundays, when he switches on the light at the crack of dawn to exercise for ten minutes.[16]

Miep and Jan had become acquainted with Dr. Pfeffer during the weekend gatherings at the Frank home; he eventually became their dentist as well. The doctor had gone into hiding alone; his fiancée was a non-Jew and the two had not been allowed to marry after the Netherlands was overrun. The once-expansive area occupied by the Franks had become cramped, but no one in the Secret Annex wanted to see anyone subjected to Nazi cruelty.

The tenants had heard from visitors how their friends and neighbors, fellow Jews, had been crowded onto Dutch streetcars, taken to the train station, and then funneled into special cars bound for they knew not where. Stories were told of how those aboard had tossed notes and cards from the windows as the train left the station in hopes that someone would direct the missives to loved ones left behind.

Fortunately for the eight souls hidden away on Princes Canal, they were surrounded by loving, caring people determined to provide for them: Miep and Jan Gies, Victor Kugler (Harry Kraler) and Johannes Kleiman (Simon Koophuis), who were charged with both the safety and the finances of those in hiding, and Bep Voskuijl (Elly Kuilmans) and her father, Johannes, who had devised a swinging bookcase that served as the door into the Secret Annex. All except Jan (who was officially a commissioner in the Frank business) worked in the office. What other employees did not know was that Otto continued to operate the company from his hiding place in the Secret Annex. For the six charged with the survival of the Franks and their friends, each day was a challenge fraught with risk and resourcefulness.

Weeks in hiding turned into months as the eight in the Secret Annex worked to keep minds sharp and fear at bay. Equally hazardous were the daily forays to find enough to feed those stowed in the attic, hidden behind Johannes Voskuijl's ingenious design.

Each morning before the other employees arrived at the office, Miep slipped up the stairs to collect the list of necessities. She would find a suitable time during the day to visit various shops to collect meat and vegetables. Bep was in charge of securing a supply of bread and milk for the hidden group. Eventually it became more difficult to provide food for the additional people with the meager supply of ration cards. Jan came up with a solution when he asked some of his underground contacts to craft fake identity cards for each of the people in the Secret Annex. These were entrusted to Miep, who used them on her daily food sorties.

Before long, Miep learned why Mr. Van Daan had her accompany him occasionally to visit the butcher shop. Upon asking for the grocery list one morning, Miep was chagrined to find the list contained various meat cuts—a commodity that was difficult to secure. When she questioned the listing, Van Daan chuckled and asked, "Remember the butcher shop off the Rozengracht where you came with me to shop?"[17] When Meip answered affirmatively, he instructed her to go back to the shop and give the list to the butcher. She was assured he would know who Miep was and for whom the goods were intended. Van Daan was correct, and she soon left the shop with a concealed bag of meat.

Mr. Van Daan also had a baker friend who had been persuaded to deliver a supply of baked goods to the office three times each week. Miep would pay him as much as possible in ration coupons, the balance to be repaid after the war. The vegetable vendor, upon becoming aware of the large amounts of produce Miep purchased weekly, began to set aside extras that would be given to her when she shopped. Even with the extra assistance from friends of those in seclusion, it became more and more difficult to provide enough food to meet the needs of ten people—the eight in the Secret Annex, plus Miep and Jan.

Before Miep and Jan married, Otto Frank had been instrumental in helping the young couple find lodging from a Jewish lady, Mrs. Stoppelman (Mrs. Samson). As the round-ups of Jewish men and women grew in the Netherlands, she began to fear for her own life and informed Miep and Jan that she was going into hiding.

While the Gieses were away for a few days, Mrs. Stoppelman simply disappeared into the underground network set up to help Jews escape Hitler's noose. The Gieses were finally apprised of her whereabouts when a letter arrived inviting them for a visit. She had been taken in by a Mrs. van der Hart. Miep and Jan packed an overnight bag and went in search of Mrs. Stoppelman. They found her ensconced in a beautiful villa in the country. Miep and Jan would soon discover that her son, Karel (Kuno van der Horst), needed a place to hide from the overbearing Nazis. A university student, Karel had been ordered to declare his allegiance to the German Reich. When he refused, he immediately became subject to arrest and incarceration. Mrs. van der Hart asked the Gieses if they would provide a safe haven for Karel. They agreed and added another person to the growing number for which food had to be found daily. Feeding her hungry charges became an unrelenting exercise in scavenging and patience. Often, meals were created from available scraps.

After returning home, an elderly Jewish man and friend of the Franks contacted Miep and asked if she and Jan could pay an urgent visit. Jan went to see him. After the two exchanged pleasantries, the man asked if a safehouse could be found for his mother. Knowing how difficult it was to find a hiding place, Jan promised only that he would try. The man excused himself and a short time later returned to the sitting room with a beautifully bound volume of Shakespeare. He then requested, "Mr. Gies, would you do me the honor to take something of mine into your home and keep it for me until after the war?"[18] Jan agreed, and although he and Miep tried, they were unable to find anyone who would assume the responsibility for the old man's mother.

The helpers who had free access to the outside world determined to spend time in the Secret Annex to try to provide some semblance of normalcy. Miep was the first to appear at the bottom of the stairs each morning to retrieve the shopping list for the day's necessities. Weekly, Jan or Miep would bring five books from the local lending library and share news of outside events with the men. Anne was often in the center of those discussions for, according to Miep, the young teen had an inquiring mind and an insatiable thirst for knowledge.

According to Glenys Roberts of the *Daily Mail*, the Gieses spent at least one night in the attic with the stowaways. Miep described the experience:

> It opened my eyes for the awful position of my friends. To live with eight people in such a small place, never being allowed to go out, never being able to talk to friends and always fearing the coming of the police.[19]

Miep was terrified as she settled into Anne's small bed with little to cushion the hard board beneath the sheets.

She relayed that she slept hardly at all, starting at each sound. The terror of being confined to the attic space was like a thick blanket of oppression settling over and around her. It was an experience she never forgot. Miep revealed later that she at last knew what it felt like to be a Jew cowering in fear of the Nazis. Anne begged Miep to move into the attic with them. She said she felt more protected with her guardian near. Miep assured the young girl that she was always in close proximity.

It was also in the fall of 1943 that Jan was recruited by a workmate to join the Resistance. After agreeing to serve in a capacity that was not only illegal but extremely risky, he was provided with instructions of what to do should he encounter trouble. Jan was taken to a local doctor, also a Resistance member, and told to go immediately to a nearby hospital for admission. It would be a safe place for him to stay until the danger passed. After about six months of activity in the group, Jan finally told Miep of his role; he hadn't wanted her to worry about his actions. Miep assured him that she was concerned, certainly, but she was pleased that he had found a way to work with the outlawed organization. A *New York Times* article said of him:

Mr. Gies, who was then a municipal welfare department employee, obtained the ration coupons his wife needed to buy the extra food for the Franks and the others . . . . Mr. Gies provided ration coupons to members of the underground resistance.

"Jan was not a person to stand in the limelight, not even amid all the publicity surrounding Anne Frank," the [Anne Frank] foundation said in a statement. "He was throughout his lifetime a man of few words, but many deeds."[20]

The winter of 1943 cast a new pall over Miep; it seemed that every Jew in their section of Amsterdam had disappeared from the streets—whether in hiding or transported to death camps, she knew not. Those in the Secret Annex were plagued daily by the fear of detection and detention, or worse. A second fear was that of disease: What would they do should someone become sick unto death? That particular anxiety became reality when Anne grew ill with a debilitating case of influenza accompanied by a bad cough. She was confined to bed and forced to stifle her coughing during the workday lest those below heard the noise from the addition. During those days of Anne's confinement in the last two months of 1943, Mr. Kleiman, Bep, and Miep became indisposed. By New Year's Day, all were recovered from their illnesses and able to celebrate the latest news—that peace would finally be achieved in 1944.

The early months of 1944 were rife with both antici-
pation and fear—hope that the Allied forces would
retake the Netherlands; fear that something would prevent
that from happening. Hope that liberation would come
before discovery; fear that their presence would be revealed.

February brought more sickness for Miep with another
attack of influenza and a bout of bronchitis. The month
also brought two more milestones—Miep celebrated her
thirty-fifth birthday, and Margot turned eighteen. It was
challenging to find ways to observe special occasions, but
they were never forgotten.

On February 15, 1944, as Miep arrived at the Secret
Annex, Petronella van Daan gently pulled her aside and
handed Miep a small package, insisting that it be opened.

Inside the makeshift wrapping, Miep found a beautiful ring of black onyx with a diamond in the center. She was stunned by the magnitude of the gift and at first refused to accept it. Mr. and Mrs. Van Daan pressed her to take the gift in sincere gratitude for all Miep had done to make life easier for the group in hiding. Miep was humbled and overwhelmed by their generosity.

The day after Easter Sunday, April 10, 1944, was to have been a holiday for the office staff; however, it proved to be very upsetting for the members of the Secret Annex as well as for Miep and Jan. The third of a series of break-ins was reported by Jo Koophuis, aka Johannes Kleiman. The Gieses raced over to the office to find the building and its inhabitants in a terrible state of affairs. A huge hole had been smashed into the front door and the contents of the building had been strewn everywhere. Repairs were made to the building, but the toll on those in residence was much more severe. Jan warned them that times were harder; thieves roamed the streets looking for anything that could be turned into a piece of bread or a guilder to purchase goods. Nothing was any longer sacred—not homes, businesses, or individuals. The fear of discovery increased exponentially.

Miep and Jan and tried to spare the attic's residents all the horrifying details of life on the streets of Amsterdam.

Weekly, more and more Jews were rounded up and transported to death camps. Jews were given a choice: deportation or sterilization. Should they choose the latter, they were assured that they would be safe following the procedure. The Nazis launched a drive to ferret out the hiding places of those who had sought refuge, promising pardon should they come forth. Fortunately, few believed that ploy. In March 1944 more Jews were arrested; insane asylums, establishments for the blind, and hospices were raided. No one was safe from the ruthlessness of the Nazis.

On June 6, 1944, Allied troops began to land on the beaches of Normandy (D-Day), and on June 12 Anne marked her fifteenth birthday. The pins on the map hung in the Secret Annex marked the progress of the Allies as they marched toward Amsterdam. The unspoken question was: Who would arrive first, the liberators or the Gestapo?

As July drew to a close, General Omar Bradley's Twelfth United States Army Group joined up with General George S. Patton, and Field Marshal Montgomery had made major inroads into the German lines. August would see an even greater fighting force as "the 12th Army Group had swollen to over 900,000 men and ultimately consisted of four field armies. It was the largest group of American soldiers to ever serve under one field commander."[21] The hiders rejoiced at the news, thinking that their liberation could not be far off. A renewed sense of excitement permeated the Secret Annex and its residents, but sadly, before the Allies could reach the outskirts of Amsterdam, disaster struck.

Friday August 4, 1944, dawned with the usual optimism that emancipation was near. Miep followed her usual custom of visiting the Secret Annex to collect the daily list of needs and was safely back at her desk before the other workers entered the doors. Just before noon, Miep raised her eyes from her work and was suddenly facing a drawn pistol held by a man in civilian clothing. With a few terse words of instruction, she realized that someone had divulged the presence of the eight concealed in the Secret Annex. Miep and her office mates, Bep Voskuijl and Johannes Kleiman, were heartbroken as their friends were led down the stairs, loaded into vehicles, and driven away. Johannes Kleiman and Victor Kugler were also arrested for their parts in aiding the Franks and their Annex mates. In the tumult that followed the search and seizure, Bep was able to slip away undetected.

After the Secret Annex had been cleared and Miep was the only one left in the office, she was challenged by Karl Silberbauer, the SS officer in charge of the raid. Miep recognized his speech pattern and accent as being the same as that of her relatives who lived in Vienna. When he stormed into her office, she challenged him with, "You are Viennese. I am from Vienna, too."[22] Silberbauer's verbal fury was unleashed on Miep as he ranted and raved about her having given aide to "Jewish garbage." Somehow she remained composed until his fury had abated and his vitriolic tongue had calmed. Finally, he said to Miep:

> From personal sympathy . . . from me personally, you can stay. But God help you if you run away. Then we take your husband . . . . I'll be back to check on you. One wrong move and off you go to prison too.[23]

Once the Nazis had departed, Miep crept upstairs to view the destruction that had enveloped the living quarters. She spied Anne's diaries and papers on the floor in the midst of the chaos, gathered them and stored them in her desk drawer—without reading them. After the Franks and their friends had entered the safe rooms, Miep had supplied Anne with notebooks to be used for her schoolwork and writings. It was these that were saved and from which *The Diary of Anne Frank* would later be compiled and published.

The following morning, Miep courageously returned to the office. As the senior member of the staff, she had to take charge of the operation. After a meeting with several of the company representatives, Miep made the decision to gather as much money as she could procure among Otto Frank's friends and offer a bribe to Viennese SS officer Silberbauer. Thinking perhaps he might listen to her plea to release the captives, she called and made an appointment with him. After speaking with him and trying to talk to his superior, Miep realized her incursion into Gestapo head-quarters was dangerous—foolhardy at its best and deadly at its worst:

> Fearing that any second I'd be grabbed by someone, I made my way back downstairs . . . . With measured steps I walked toward the door to the building. Gestapo were everywhere in the corridors, like flies in fancy uniforms. Again the thought rang in my brain: *People who enter this building do not always come out again.* I put one foot in front of the other, waiting for someone to stop me.
>
> Back out in the street, I was amazed at how easy it had been to walk out the door.[24]

Thwarted by her attempt to secure the freedom of her friends, she returned home. In late September 1944, Bep's father, Johannes, suddenly returned. The officials at the camp in which he had been incarcerated had freed him because of his health. Miep was overjoyed to see him and delighted to relinquish the daily company operations to him. Then, realizing the danger that both she and Jan faced, Miep advised their houseguest, Karel, to return home to Hilversum, promising he could return to Amsterdam as soon as it was safe.

One month later, a BBC broadcast informed the Dutch that Allied troops had reached the town of Breda in the south. As the beaten and bedraggled German army began to retreat, it was followed by collaborators who had worked with the Nazis during the occupation. From secret hiding places, the Dutch flag appeared, but the celebration was short-lived as word spread that the announcement was false. Hearts and hopes dropped as the Germans returned to Amsterdam.

The search for food simply to survive became a daily trial. Often Miep and the wife of one of the employees had to ride their coveted bicycles far into the countryside just to gather a few carrots, beets, and potatoes to keep Jan and her alive. The peril to two women traveling in the early morning hours was unnerving, but together they managed to scavenge enough commodities to keep them alive. Looking

around at the cruel signs of starvation, lack, and deprivation, it was clearly understood that the Nazis were using
all means possible to meet their own needs and that Miep's
beloved adopted homeland and its people had been sorely
ravaged by the five-year occupation.

5

In May 1945, the Canadians marched into Amsterdam, a sign that with the deaths of Adolf Hitler and Benito Mussolini, and the surrender of the German army, the war had finally ended. Throughout the Netherlands, attempts were being made to rebuild structures, roads, and rail lines. Allied planes began to drop food supplies at Schiphol Airport, and later across the town. Shops remained empty for some time, but slowly goods and services returned to the country.

Once the Allies had moved into Amsterdam, Victor Kugler came out of hiding. He had been sent, along with Johannes, to Amersfoort, a camp that housed political prisoners, those who had concealed Jews, and traders on the black market. He had managed to escape from a group being transferred to a camp inside Germany and made his way home. Victor's wife had kept him hidden all those months.

As Jews liberated from concentration camps began to sift back into Amsterdam, Jan and Miep would inquire about the Frank family—Otto, Edith, Margot, and Anne. No one had ever heard of them. Finally one person responded, "Mister, I have just seen Otto Frank and he is coming back!"[25] Several days later the two old friends stood face-to-face, Otto carrying a small bundle of belongings—all he had managed to hoard from his months in captivity. The two friends embraced as tears flowed. Otto was finally able to speak as he sadly relayed the information that Miep did not want to hear: Edith had perished in the concentration camp shortly before liberating forces reached its gates.

Upon his return to Amsterdam, Otto took up residence with Miep and Jan. He began writing letters to individuals he knew who had been at Bergen-Belsen while his girls were there; he scrutinized lists of survivors posted in the city. From one list he learned that Dr. Pfeffer (Albert Dussel) had perished in the Neuengamme concentration camp. The elder van Daan had perished at either Buchenwald or Theresienstadt, and Peter had been killed on the very day Mauthausen was liberated by the Allies. But no one knew of the whereabouts of Margot and Anne. Finally one morning while opening the daily mail in the office, Otto Frank slit open an envelope and removed the folded page inside. He called out to Miep in an utterly atonal voice, and when she turned it was to see his stricken face. Breathing raggedly and in great anguish he told her that a nurse in Rotterdam had written that neither Margot nor Anne had survived. Both had died of typhus, a disease transmitted by lice; Margot first, and then Anne.

As Otto sank into the chair in his office, head bowed in total dejection, Miep slipped to her desk. Opening the drawer in which Anne's papers had been stashed, she emptied it and reverently carried them into Otto Frank's office, where she laid them on his desk. Realizing the treasure that had been presented him, Otto closed his door and began to read.

After he moved in with the Gieses, Otto began to collect the possessions he had entrusted to others when he and his family went into hiding. He presented Edith's antique writing desk to Miep, as well as other treasured items. A friend in England sent Otto two new bicycles, one of which he gave to Miep. Another friend in the United States sent a gift package with cocoa powder, a treat about which Miep had dreamed during the cold, dark, hungry months of deprivation under the Nazis.

Otto began to translate segments of Anne's diary and papers for his mother who lived in Basel, Switzerland. He would frequently offer them to Miep to read, but she would always decline. As the small, newly formed family began to entertain friends once again, Otto mentioned during one Sunday afternoon gathering that he had his daughter's diary. A man in attendance asked to be allowed to read it and after completion suggested that her father publish Anne's writings. Otto finally agreed to publish a small portion of her private papers. Still, he pressed Miep to read the work, but both she and Jan continued to decline. She finally relented and in one sitting, alone in her room, read the book from cover to cover. Miep's reaction:

> From the first word, I heard Anne's voice come back to speak to me from where she had gone. I lost track of time. Anne's voice tumbled out of the book, so full of life, moods, curiosity, feelings. She was no longer gone and destroyed. She was alive again in my mind.[26]

The diary was eventually translated into English and published in the United States. The publication was soon followed by a stage play and a movie, all based on the thoughts and activities of a young girl who had been forced into hiding—all because of the hatefulness of anti-Semitism.

In 1950, as the Netherlands began to return to normalcy, Miep gave birth to a son, Paul. Two years later, Otto Frank emigrated to Switzerland and found a lovely lady with whom to share his life. She, too, had been arrested and taken to Auschwitz, where she lost her family with the exception of one daughter.

The question of who had betrayed the Franks and their friends in the Secret Annex has never been answered. Jemma Saunders wrote of several possibilities for the History in an Hour website:

> . . . residents were wary of one Willem van Maaren, who replaced the previous warehouse manager when he became ill. Van Maaren was intensely curious about the rooms at the back of the building and noticed that unusually large amounts of food were delivered to the premises. He purposefully left traps downstairs, supposedly to catch thieves, and asked the office staff uncomfortable questions. When questioned about the betrayal in 1948 and 1964,

he admitted his suspicions but denied informing the Gestapo. . . .

In her 1998 biography of Anne, Melissa Müller pointed a finger at Lena van Bladeren-Hartog, a cleaner at 263 Prinsengracht whose husband worked in the warehouse. Lena gossiped with another woman that there were Jews hiding in the building and there are rumours that it was a woman who telephoned the Gestapo. Tonny Ahlers was, according to biographer Carol Ann Lee, a vicious anti-Semite who blackmailed Otto Frank both during and after the war. Records testify that Ahlers betrayed several Jews during the Occupation and was also arrested for other crimes. According to Ahlers' brother and children, he admitted betraying the Franks; however no official records verify this and his death in 2000 halted any further enquiry.

The 2003 investigation concluded that, while the case against Ahlers was strong, all evidence was circumstantial. Along with Lena van Bladeren-Hartog and Willem van Maaren, his name was cleared.[27]

Miep's final word on who betrayed the group hidden in the Secret Annex: "We shall never know."[28]

From those who gave her succor in her early years, the caring family with whom she lived in Amsterdam, Miep Gies learned love and tolerance, compassion and empathy. Having been the recipient of the gifts of benevolence, charity, tenderness, and understanding from others, she was able to unselfishly return that favor to Jews who were in danger, as did a myriad of ordinary people—teachers, lawyers, magistrates, businessmen, physicians, housewives, farmers, and laborers.

The figures of the number who perished in the Netherlands is staggering:

Of the 140,000 Jews who had lived in the Netherlands before 1940, only 30,000 (21%) survived the war. But the real picture was even worse than this suggests. The Netherlands had the highest Jewish death toll of any western European country. Of the approximately 107,000 Jews deported to the camps, only 5000 survived; a survival rate of less than 5%.... This high death toll had a number of reasons. One was the excellent state of Dutch civil records: the Dutch state, before the war, had recorded substantial information on every Dutch national. This allowed the Nazi regime to determine easily who was Jewish (whether fully or partly of Jewish ancestry) simply by accessing the data.[29]

Miep and Jan Gies were designated Righteous Among the Nations on March 8, 1972, and were inducted into Yad Vashem (the Holocaust Martyrs' and Heroes' Remembrance Authority in Jerusalem), Israel's official memorial to Holocaust victims. Jan Gies—husband, father, Resistance fighter, and friend—died of kidney failure on January 26, 1993. Miep Gies—wife, mother, courageous ally, and colleague—died at the age of 100 on January 11, 2010.

OSKAR SCHINDLER

*"I hated the brutality, the sadism, and the insanity
of Nazism. I just couldn't stand by and see people
destroyed. I did what I could, what I had to do,
what my conscience told me I must do. That's
all there is to it. Really, nothing more."*

—OSKAR SCHINDLER

The scene: Poland 1939. The order of the day: brutality. Atrocities abounded, and sadism ruled. The decimation of the Jewish population had not begun overnight. Author Peter Longerich gives us a glimpse of the process for the rabid anti-Semitism that held Eastern Europe in its grasp during World War II:

> The field of *Judenpolitik* did not develop autonomously or independently, but functioned within a context determined by the other areas of political activity. It penetrated them and radically transformed them. The National Socialists tended to understand traditional political fields (such as foreign, social, and labour policy) in a

racist manner and to redefine them along racist lines. Their starting point was the assumption that there was something akin to 'an international Jewish problem' that foreign policy had to focus on; they assumed that social policy in the Nazi state took the form of welfare provision for 'Aryans' alone and not for the 'racially inferior' . . . Jewish labour was essentially unproductive and parasitic and therefore, as a matter of principal, only used Jewish people for particularly onerous and humiliating physical work . . . . anti-Semitism always played a major role.[30]

The entire nation was in the grasp of merciless barbarianism. Into this fray stepped an unlikely and flawed hero—Oskar Schindler. Eastern Europe was shrouded in the darkness of death; Schindler was a flickering candle. You may recognize his name from the Academy Award–winning film directed by Steven Spielberg, *Schindler's List*. Schindler's wife, Emilie, wrote of that time in her memoir, *Where Light and Shadow Meet*:

Stephen Spielberg's film, Thomas Keneally's book [*Schindler's Ark*], and all the rivers of ink

spilled fifty years after the facts depict my husband as a hero for this century. This is not true.
He was not a hero, and neither was I. We only
did what we had to.[31]

"Unremarkable" describes the early childhood of the man
whose name would become a household word in 1994 with
the release of Spielberg's film. Oskar was born to Johann
(Hans and Franziska (Luser) Schindler on April 28, 1908 in
Zwittau, Austria-Hungary, now Svitavy, Czechoslovakia.
His schooling sped along fairly smoothly until young Oskar
enrolled in a technical school after finishing his secondary
education. He had been caught falsifying information on his
performance evaluation and was disqualified. When he did
return, it was not to continue on to university, but to learn
machines and chauffeuring.

Oskar met his future wife, Emilie Pelzl, while he was
making and selling farm machinery with his father. On
March 6, 1928, after a year's courtship, the two married and
the newlyweds moved in with his parents in Zwittau. There
they would remain for seven years. Their marriage would
be challenged by Oskar's inability to keep a job and by two
traits he had learned from his father: drinking and woman-
izing. As Emilie hinted rather overtly in her memoir—even

our heroes are sometimes flawed. After working for a time with his father, Oskar took up motorcycle racing. He proudly sped around the country on his 250 cm Konigsswellen Moto-Guzzi, but his failure to ever finish first quickly took the luster off his hobby. Oskar soon ended his racing pursuits.

His business career was checkered, his earlier attempts to earn a living cut short by a stretch in the Czechoslovak military. Oskar's failure to provide for his wife caused great frustration in their marriage. Emilie had brought what was a sizeable dowry at the time (100,000 Czech crowns—$2,964 American) with her. Oskar had exhausted the funds on a fancy automobile, among other extravagances. His new wife was not pleased with Oskar's actions.

After only eighteen months in the army, the restless young man returned to his previous employer, Moravian Electrotechnic, only to be sidelined again when the company faced bankruptcy. After a year of unemployment, Oskar landed a job with the Bank of Prague that would last until 1938. During that period, he was detained several times for public inebriation. The old saying "like father, like son" certainly applied to the Schindler men. Oskar, taking a page from his father's profligate lifestyle, had an affair with a childhood friend with whom he had a son and daughter. In 1935, the elder Schindler deserted his wife; she died several months later after what had been a prolonged illness.

History has proven that the young Schindler became a true hero, but as we have seen, his early life held no clue of what was to come. Yet he would display an intensity of bravery, audacity, and compassion unique for the period in which he dwelled.

At the age of twenty-seven, he enlisted in the Sudeten German Party in Czechoslovakia. Its aim was to divide the country and force its inhabitants into uniting with Hitler's Third Reich. Oskar became an operative for the Abwehr, a Nazi spy agency, and was stationed in Breslau. His duty, other than recruiting individuals for the organization, was to gather reliable information regarding military bases and troops, railway installations, and any other data that might be deemed pertinent.

It was an alliance that Schindler would downplay following the end of the war and one that placed him in jeopardy in his homeland. As a spy, he discovered just how hazardous his job could be when on July 18, 1938, Oskar was arrested for espionage and taken to the National Police Office. He was assured of excellent treatment if he would only confess to his crimes against the state; Schindler acquiesced and was incarcerated, but for less than three months.

He was saved by the Munich Agreement, which called for "a settlement permitting Nazi Germany's annexation of portions of Czechoslovakia along the country's borders mainly inhabited by German speakers."[32]

Author David M. Crowe writes of Schindler's involvement with the spy network:

> More than likely, Schindler never fully left Abwehr . . . . the fact that Abwehr sent him on a special mission to Turkey in 1940 indicates the great trust that [Abwehr chief Wilhelm] Canaris' organization put in his skills.[33]

In January 1939, and following his release, Oskar and Emilie were sent to the city of Moravska Ostrava, now in the Czech Republic, to provide information germane to Hitler's take-over of Bohemia and Moravia. Emilie would remain there even after Oskar's later move to Poland.

It seems certain, however, that Oskar continued his efforts for the organization during the planning stages of the invasion of Poland. The Germans were specifically interested in data related to the rail line through Jablunkov Pass, an essential site for the successful movement of German troops into the region.

Hitler signed off on instructions for the invasion of Poland on the last day of August 1939. Seventeen hours after the ink had dried, the Nazi army and five Abwehr commando groups had swarmed over the border into Poland. This was despite demands by the British and French to withdraw as a lead-in to peace negotiations. Hitler rejected all demands for talks and the two nations declared war on the Führer and his Third Reich (Great German Realm) on September 3. By the sixth of October, German troops had defeated the Polish army and were in firm control of the country.

One of the first cities captured by the Nazis was Kraków, and it was to there that Schindler was dispatched in late 1939. It was his plan to reenergize his flagging business career. He would soon discover that Hitler had other, more depraved, plans for the city and its people.

According to Crowe:

> On August 22, Hitler told his top generals to "act brutally" towards all Poles. The Fuhrer viewed Poland's Jews "as the most horrible thing imaginable." Hitler added that the aim of the war was physically to annihilate the enemy, in this case the Poles. His special *Einsatz* [paramilitary death] squads had "orders mercilessly

and pitilessly to send men, women, and children of Polish extraction and language to their death." . . . . an orgy of atrocities followed; it put earlier Nazi brutalities in the Greater Reich "completely in the shade."[34]

In October 1939, Oskar rented an apartment in Kraków and a month later hired Mila Pfefferberg as an interior designer to decorate his new home. She was the mother of Poldek Pfefferberg, a young man skilled in black market transactions. He would not only be essential to Schindler's efforts to save Jews from the Nazis' Final Solution but would become a lifelong friend.

In an interview after the war, Pfefferberg revealed the promise by Schindler that he would safeguard those who worked for him as much as possible; he would provide shelter, sustenance, and clothing for them. This he did.

According to Pfefferberg:

> Oscar Schindler was a modern Noah . . . he saved individuals, husbands and wives and their children, families. It was like the saying: To save one life is to save the whole world. Schindler called us his children. In 1944, he was a very wealthy man, a multimillionaire. He could have

taken the money and gone to Switzerland . . . he could have bought Beverly Hills. But instead, he gambled his life and all of his money to save us.[35]

After the war, Pfefferberg made a promise to himself: He would tell the story of Oskar Schindler to anyone who would listen. He vowed that the world would know that "even on the days when the air was black with the ashes from bodies on fire, there was hope in Kraków because Oscar Schindler was there."[36]

S chindler met Itzhak Stern in November 1939. Stern was a Polish Jew whose property had been seized by Abwehr envoy Josef Aue. When the Nazis marched into Poland, all Jewish property was confiscated—businesses, residences, belongings. Jews were divested of all freedoms under Reich domination.[37] The concept of Judenpolitik, or anti-Jewish laws, overshadowed every Jewish man, woman, and child in the country.

Schindler soon approached Stern for advice concerning the acquisition of a factory where enamel kitchenware had been produced. Its owners were forced to relinquish control to the German occupational forces' Trusteeship Authority, and Oskar petitioned for the role of trustee. He took control of the Rekord Company in an area of Kraków.

It was renamed *Deutsche Emailewaren Fabrik* and was simply called Emalia. Originally he employed only Polish laborers, but as he began to comprehend the worsening plight of the Jews in the country, the scales began to tip in favor of Jews engaged to work in the factory.

Oskar petitioned for permission to produce ammunition shells, and later cookware for German troops, an act that would allow the factory to be categorized as a vital part of manufacturing goods for the war effort. His request was granted, and he called on former owner Abraham Bankier to assist him with the business. Schindler effectively saved the lives of his Jewish employees by convincing the Nazi SS that his workers were a vital part of the combat strategy.

An edict demanding that all Jews leave Kraków within fourteen days was enacted on August 1, 1940. Those who were gainfully employed would be allowed to remain but only if their jobs were war-related. By March 1941, only about 15,000 of the original approximately 80,000 Jews remained in the city. They were soon forced into the Kraków Ghetto, which had been instituted in Podgórze, the manufacturing district.[38]

There were apparently several coincidences that led Oskar to think about the well-being of his factory workers, but in the beginning he was only concerned with the income-producing aspects of the business. He hired Jews because they worked more cheaply than did their Polish counterparts—the pittance established by the Nazis occupying the city. Crowe asked the question, "Were there other factors that might have affected Schindler's drift into a more protective attitude toward his Jewish workers, particularly in 1942?"[39] The answer begins, perhaps, with Oskar's arrest by the dreaded Gestapo near the end of 1941 for "fraternizing with Jews and Poles."[40] He was placed in a cell at Montelupich Prison, a terrifying place of confinement.

Oskar devised a means to let his friends know his whereabouts; and that—even from inside his cell—led to his release after a five-day stay. Apparently, Schindler knew the value of a good bottle of vodka placed in the right hands. It would not be the first time, or the last, that he would employ bribes and black-market gifts to gain an edge with the Nazi regime. In his book, *The Book of the Just: The Unsung Heroes Who Rescued Jews from Hitler*, Eric Silver wrote of the Gestapo barging into Schindler's plant and demanding that he relinquish a family that had been accused of obtaining counterfeit papers. According to Schindler, "Three hours after they walked in, two drunken Gestapo men reeled out of my office without their prisoners and without the incriminating documents they had demanded."[41]

Oskar was also impacted by the arrests of fourteen of his Jewish workers. According to Crowe:

> There was no science to the last roundup in the Kraków ghetto in the summer of 1942. It is quite possible that Bankier and the other Schindlerjuden [Schindler's Jews] were picked up by the Germans even though they had Blauschein [identity cards]. Given Oskar's earlier problems with the Gestapo, it is possible that the Gestapo picked up Bankier and the other Schindler Jews as a warning to Schindler.... Whatever prompted the attempted deportation of Schindler's fourteen Jewish workers, his dramatic intervention at the Prokocim train station on June 8 saved them from certain death.... Almost losing the irreplaceable Abraham Bankier to the Gestapo must have had a tremendous impact on Oskar.... what impact did the June 1942 deportations have on his decision to commit his resources totally to this effort?[42]

The Kraków Ghetto existed for only two years before being methodically cleared of its inhabitants. It was purged in three cycles: The first transpired in May 1942 when everyone who did not possess an identity card—about 4,000 individuals—was sent to the Belzec death camp. Five days later, on June 4, another 600 Jews were randomly gunned down in the streets of the slum. By month's end, the Nazis had successfully diminished the size of the ghetto, forcing the residents into a smaller zone.

Another episode that nudged Oskar to be more diligent about saving the lives of his Jewish employees was the opening of the Plaszow concentration camp in 1942. Located near the city center of Kraków, its commandant, Amon Göth, was a sadistic murderer. It was said that "he would never start his breakfast without shooting at least one person."[43] Apparently, the vicious butcher was not above using ghetto children for target practice during his rounds. Göth demanded that all manufacturing facilities be relocated inside the camp. Schindler diplomatically bribed the senior officer into allowing him to build a camp subsidiary on the grounds of Emalia. Unknown to Goth, the Jews would be cared for and kept safe in the facility.

By the end of the year, the remaining area was divided into Ghetto A, reserved for the work force, and Ghetto B for all other Jews. March 1943 saw "A" completely shuttered and its residents taken away to the Plaszow concentration camp. The following day, March 14, those in "B" were murdered wherever found; only a few hundred escaped instant death. Their reprieve was short lived, for they were carried off to Auschwitz, from where few escaped death. Tadeusz Pankiewicz, a Polish Roman Catholic pharmacist who was allowed to practice within the confines of the ghetto, described the horror:

> The ghetto echoed with shots; the dead and wounded fell; blood marked the German crimes in the street . . . . People, weakened by heat and thirst, fainted and fell. In front of the pharmacy there was a small army car to which every few minutes the SS men brought valises filled with valuables taken during the searches of the deportees. They took everything from them . . . . Some of the unfortunates looked at those waiting their turns, resignation and apathy etched on their faces. These people were already beyond feeling.[44]

As these events preyed on Schindler's mind, his life was highly impacted by yet another factor—that one centered on a *Kinderheim*—a children's home established by the Nazis. Jewish parents were informed that their children up to age fourteen could be dropped off at the home while they went on to work. There the youngsters would receive excellent care and nourishment. Each day, the home was filled with many children, but the respite lasted only a short time. One black day Nazi troopers entered the home and slaughtered every child. The ruthless attack was only one of the incidents that transformed Oskar Schindler.

Commandant Göth must have been in his heartless element when called upon to empty the ghetto in March 1943. The residents were classified by their ability to work; those deemed incapable were both transported to Belzec and immediately gassed or to Auschwitz, or summarily executed on the spot. Rena Ferber, one survivor, was shocked by the brutality of the female SS guards:

> When we were loaded on the train in Plaszów, an SS woman hit me on the head. They were so vicious and brutal and sadistic, more than men. I think because some of them were women and you expect kindness, it was shocking. But of course, some were fat and big and ugly.[45]

Rena was later spared execution by a Nazi guard who accused her of breaking a machine in Schindler's factory. She crouched, terrified before the guard whose pistol was pointed at her head. Oskar interceded and pointed out that a small child could not break the huge piece of equipment. Rena said of Schindler:

> I would not be alive today if it wasn't for Oscar Schindler, my Mother survived and so did my grandfather. It's a tragedy that Oscar Schindler died young before the world could acknowledge his heroism.[46]

Göth was accused of stealing Jewish belongings, considered by the SS to be property of the Nazi state, and was removed from his post on September 13, 1944. He was also charged with failure to properly care for the prisoners in his care, but charges against him were later dropped. In 1945, Göth was discovered in a mental institution and arrested by US troops. He was returned to Poland, tried as a war criminal, and hanged.

While Göth was facing his own demons at the hands of the SS, Schindler learned that the Nazis were shuttering plants not totally engaged in war-related endeavors. He ordered production lines to abandon the manufacture of enamel products and to immediately begin fabricating anti-tank grenades. Also designed to protect his workers, Oskar received permission to move the plant to Brunnlitz,

Czechoslovakia. He took with him over one thousand Jews from Kraków and enroute liberated another eighty-five from a Nazi labor camp, but the trip was not without terror for Schindler's men and women. While making preparations for the move, Oskar had ordered the preparation of his famous "list," which included the names of 1,100 Jews.

The men bound for Schindler's new plant were loaded aboard a train bound initially for the Gross-Rosen concentration camp; the women went to Auschwitz-Birkenau—a death camp. Once inside the camp gates, the men were forced to disrobe, then ordered to stand outdoors in freezing weather. They were subjected to the typical Nazi dehumanizing procedures—cavity searches, deluged with disinfectants, and having their heads shaved by Russian barbers before being allowed to don used clothing. They were herded into overcrowded barracks before being subjected to regular brutality. Crowe described a typical day for Schindler's men:

> Beatings by the *Stubendienst*, the German criminal prisoners assigned to guard the

Schindler men, took place constantly. Few of the Schindler men escaped beatings by these sadists. The SS established a strict regimen of military-style calisthenics for the prisoners. After roll call at 8:00 AM, they were taken to a ditch; here they had two minutes to relieve themselves, their only chance to do this . . . After breakfast, they exercised until noon and then had an hour for lunch. They had calisthenics again in the afternoon and were then locked in their barracks for the night.[47]

The ordeal of the women lasted three long, brutal weeks. When they boarded the railcars to Brinnlitz, none were aware that there would be an interim stop at the death camp where the possibility of being gassed hovered over the terrified captives. Upon arrival, they were forced off the train to face SS guards and snarling Alsatian guard dogs. Again, Crowe describes their entry:

After stripping, they were subjected to "gynecological examination," the full shaving of all body hair with a dull razor and scissors, and a bath "under streams of boiling hot or freezing water." . . . delousing consisted of hitting each woman on her newly bald head with a "stinking rag that made every shaved place burn, whatever it was, carbolic acid or something."[48]

As the men had done, the women were forced to stand outside, shivering in the October cold. The stench from the smoke hanging over the camp was sickening. Tired, hungry, and thirsty, women tried to catch snowflakes on their tongues to alleviate their thirst, only to discover that the flakes were ashes pouring from the smokestacks of the crematorium. The female guards took exception to the idea that Schindler's women were only in the camp temporarily and made their daily lives a living hell. The prisoners were punished for even the smallest infraction of convoluted camp regulations. After three horrifying weeks, the women were released to travel to Brunnlitz. Schindler's friend Itzhak Stern supplied the narrative:

We [the men] arrived in Brunnlitz in October 1944. Several days later the women hadn't yet arrived, despite the authorized list. My friends induced me to turn to Schindler to expedite their arrival. At the same time Schindler's secretary entered. He looked at the pretty young woman, pointed at a large diamond on the ring on his finger and said "do you want this diamond?" The young woman got excited. Schinder told her "take the list of the Jewish women, put the best food and drink in your suitcase and go to Auschwitz. You know, the commander there likes pretty girls. When you return and once the women arrive, you will get the diamond and more." The secretary went on her way. When two days passed and she hadn't returned, Schindler took [a man identified only as] Major Platte with him and went to Auschwitz. A few days later all the women—the wives, mothers and sisters of the men—arrived. Only my own mother was missing.[49]

This group was the only one to be shipped *out* of Auschwitz during the Holocaust. Their survival was solely due to Schindler's intervention. The women were once again loaded onto railcars and began their frantic and anxious flight to Brunnlitz. En route they were denied food and water, and feared the worst each time the train stopped along the way. After some time, the train came to a halt and the women were ordered to disembark. The Shoah website gives us this understanding of those liberated from Auschwitz:

> When the women arrived to the factory in Brunnlitz, weak, hungry, frostbitten, less than human, Oscar Schindler met them in the courtyard. They never forgot the sight of Schindler standing in the doorway. And they never forgot his raspy voice when he—surrounded by SS guards—gave them an unforgettable guarantee: "Now you are finally with me, you are safe now. Don't be afraid of anything. You don't have to worry anymore."[50]

Another survivor on the list was Stella Müller-Madej. Only fourteen years old when she began working for Oskar, he listed her as being sixteen and a metal worker. She later revealed:

> What I'll say is nothing poetic, but I will repeat till the end of my days that the first time I was given life by my parents and the second time by Oscar Schindler. In '44 there were around 700 women transported from Płaszów, 300 of whom were on his list, and he fought

for us like a lion, because they didn't want to let us out of Auschwitz. He was offered better and healthier "material" from new transports, unlike us, who had spent several years in the camp. But he got us out . . . he saved us.[51]

It was in Brunnlitz that Oskar reunited with his wife, Emilie. She is credited with scrounging enough food to feed the workers that Schindler transferred from the Kraków plant. Although she was largely ignored in the film *Schindler's List*, historians have written of her efforts:

Even today surviving Schindler-Jews remember how Emilie worked indefatigably to secure food and somehow managed to provide the sick with extra nourishment and apples . . . . Until the liberation of spring, 1945, the Schindler's used all means at their disposal to ensure the safety of the Schindler-Jews. They spent every Pfennig [penny] they had, and even Emilie's jewels were sold, to buy food, clothes, and medicine. They set up a secret sanatorium in the factory with medical equipment purchased on the black market. Here Emilie looked after the sick. Those who did not survive were given a fitting Jewish burial in a hidden graveyard—established and paid for by the Schindlers . . . . One night in the last weeks of the war a tireless Emilie . . . saved 250 Jews from impending death. Emilie was confronted by Nazis transporting the Jews, crowded into four wagons, from Golleschau to a death camp. She succeeded in persuading the Gestapo to send these Jews to the factory camp . . . In her *A Memoir* by Erika Rosenberg she recalls:

> " . . . It was impossible to distinguish the men from the women: they were all so emaciated—weighing under seventy pounds most of them, they looked like skeletons . . . ."

Throughout that night and for many nights following, Emilie worked without halt on the frozen and starved skeletons . . . . Three more men died, but with the care, the warmth, the milk and the medicine, the others gradually rallied. After the war survivors told about Emilie's unforgettable heroism....[52]

Once the men and women had recovered from their horrific ordeal, Oskar and Emilie made certain they were given light duties in order to regain strength and recuperate.

The Brunnlitz factory was tasked with manufacturing shell casings for the German military, but according to the Holocaust Research Project:

> In all that time not one useable shell was produced, not one shell passed the quality tests performed by the military. Instead, false military travel passes and ration cards were produced, as well as the collection of Nazi uniforms, weapons and ammunition.[53]

As long as he employed Jewish workers at his Brinnlitz factory, Oskar was required to pay the SS a sum for each man and woman, a total of $1,600 to $2,400 per day. He estimated that over a seven-month period before the end of the war, he had grudgingly added hundreds of thousands of dollars to Nazi coffers. Although he had no work for some of the women who spent the day knitting or sewing, still he paid the amount demanded to guarantee their safety and survival. Schindler's bid to protect the Jews under his authority spread to trying to secure enough rations to feed them and the SS contingent assigned to his sub-camp. While it was still a concentration camp, it was free of the random inhumaneness and hostility many had suffered at the hands of Göth in Kraków. Their world was rocked when in the early months of 1945 the feared commandant appeared at Brunnlitz. Göth had made the visit to be assured that the booty he had confiscated from Jews in the ghetto—sixty boxes of which he had sent to the new camp with Oskar— had not been lost. Fortunately his visit was short, and Göth would not be seen again by the majority of Jewish workers; he was convicted of war crimes and hanged following the war.

On April 29, 1945, Adolf Hitler married his mistress, Eva Braun. The following day the two committed suicide as the Russian Army bore down on Czechoslovakia. Oskar and Emilie climbed into his two-seater Horch, a German-made vehicle, and fled from the Soviets. During the journey, the vehicle and a truck bearing his mistress and a load of Schindler's possessions were confiscated by the occupying troops. A large diamond hidden in the front seat for future funds was lost to the marauding Russians. Bereft of his fortune, Schindler and his group eventually escaped to Switzerland and settled in Bavaria in late 1945; he estimated that over one million dollars had been spent to support his workers. When the conflict ended for Oskar and his beloved *Schindlerjuden*, he had become a most implausible role model. He had begun the war as a multimillionaire war racketeer; when it ended, he was penniless and had risked his own life to save the Jews under his protection. He was reduced to depending on various Jewish organizations and donations from his *Schindlerjuden* to survive.

Several years later, Schindler was interviewed by author Herbert Steinhouse, who wrote:

> Schindler's exceptional deeds stemmed from just that elementary sense of decency and humanity that our sophisticated age seldom sincerely believes in. A repentant opportunist saw the light and rebelled against the sadism and vile criminality all around him.[54]

Like many Nazi Party members, Schindler and his wife, Emilie, emigrated to South America in 1949 and settled in Argentina. He tried his hand at raising chickens and then nutria (at one time prized for their fur); neither was successful. He then returned to Germany and lived for years in obscure poverty.

A tree was planted in the Avenue of the Righteous at Yad Vashem in 1962 to honor Schindler for his efforts to rescue Jews during the Holocaust. While preparing the information for the Yad Vashem committee, several Schindler Jews wrote:

> We cannot forget the sorrow of Egypt, we cannot forget Haman [ancient Persian official who plotted to kill Jews but was stopped by Esther and hanged], we cannot forget Hitler. But we also cannot forget the just among the unjust; remember Oskar Schindler.[55]

On the night of Oskar's induction, Dr. Moshe Bejski, an Israeli lawyer and judge, recounted his experiences as a Schindler Jew. He told of many incidents surrounding his benefactor. He ended his testimony before the august crowd with "Not a thing you and your wife have done for us have we forgotten, nor shall we ever forget as long as we live."[56]

As a side note, Bejski was called upon by Prosecutor Gideon Hausner to testify against Adolf Eichmann during the Nazi's trial in Israel. Bejski's account of the Plaszow camp revealed the hopelessness, helplessness, and horror of the camp. He was also able to relate the despair felt by Schindler's workers when they learned their protector had been arrested by the SS and their delight when he was released.

In 1966, Oskar was awarded the German Order of Merit. He died on October 9, 1974; his body was transported to Jerusalem where he was buried in the Catholic Cemetery on Mount Zion.

Emilie opted to remain in Argentina. In 1993, both Oskar and Emilie were honored as Righteous Among the Nations. That same year, the United States Holocaust Memorial Council posthumously bestowed its Medal of Remembrance on Schindler. This decoration gives tribute to the men and women who exhibited exceptional acts of bravery during the Holocaust. The medal was presented to Emilie Schindler. She resided just outside Buenos Aires until her death in 2001 at the age of 94.

Director Steven Spielberg bought the rights to Thomas Keneally's novel *Schindler's Ark,* and in 1993 co-produced the story of Oskar Schindler, renaming it *Schindler's List*. It was a box office and budgetary success, having made $321.3 million, and garnered seven Academy Awards, including one for Spielberg.

There was a fictitious scene in the movie, based on the presentation of a ring to Schindler; it had supposedly been made from the gold fillings of one of the factory worker's teeth. Engraved on the ring were words from the *Talmud*, "Whoever saves one life saves a world entire." Scratched inside the band was a simple message: "Thank you." In the movie script, a grief-stricken Schindler responds, "I could have got more out.... I could have got more ... if I'd just ... I could have got more.... I didn't do enough!" (He rips the swastika pin from his lapel and holds it aloft.) "This pin, two people. This is gold. Two more people. He would have given me two for it, at least one."[57]

Oskar Schindler is credited with saving the lives of at least 1,100, and some say 1,200 Jewish men, women, and children. His list is preserved in the archives of Yad Vashem in Jerusalem.

Author David M. Crowe, who spent seven years documenting the life of Schindler, said of Oskar's relationship with the Schindler Jews:

> Most of them were well aware of Oskar's human flaws but put these moral qualms aside when it came to judging him. They felt he deserved all the accolades that the modern world has to offer.[58]

IRENA SENDLER

"If someone is drowning, you have to give them your hand. When the war started, all of Poland was drowning in a sea of blood, and those who were drowning the most were the Jews. And among the Jews, the worst off were the children. So I had to give them my hand."[59]

—IRENA SENDLER

O ne year after the birth of Miep Gies in Vienna, Austria, on February 15, 1910, a baby girl was born to Dr. Stanislaw and Janina Krzyżanowska, near Warsaw Poland. Her name was Irena, and she, like Miep, would make a difference in the lives of Jews targeted by Adolf Hitler's quest for his infamous Final Solution.

Irena's father, a physician, frequently cared for patients who could not afford to pay for his services. A group of his relatives offered a building to house a hospital in a small village near Warsaw. There, Stanislaw was able to treat those with diseases such as tuberculosis. In the midst of the deprivation following World War I, a typhus epidemic broke out. Dr. Krzyżanowska was one of the few physicians in the vicinity willing to make house calls to treat the ill and soon caught the disease. Tragically, just seven years after she was born, Irena's father died. Her mother, Janina, continued to operate the facility for three years. Irena said later:

> My father died when I was seven, but I'll always remember him saying that people are divided into good and bad. Nationality, religion or race mean nothing: what kind of person you are is all that counts.[60]

As devastating as typhus was in 1917, it would be eclipsed the following year by the pandemic of Spanish Influenza, a deadly virus that took the lives of twenty million people worldwide. It claimed more than the total number of combat deaths during World War I. Irena was one of the lucky ones—she survived the flu. One of the treatments used to relieve the pain of the headaches caused by high fever was the practice called "trepanning." A hole was drilled in the patient's skull to relieve pressure in the cranium. As a result of the treatment, Irena was left with blinding migraine headaches that continued throughout most of her life. Despite the fact that a vaccination against typhus was found during World War II, and even though the disease has largely been eradicated in more advanced countries, it does still pose a problem for underprivileged nations in

Asia, Africa, and South America where outbreaks continue to occur.

Irena's first brush with the anti-Semitism that would eventually grip the continent in a stranglehold was at Warsaw University, where she studied Polish Literature. There, the *ghetto lawkowe*, or bench system—a means of blatant segregation of Jewish students—had become popular. Jews were forced to sit on the left side of classrooms and were randomly targeted with violent acts. In protest of that practice, Irena sometimes sat with the Jewish students, and when finally challenged, she mutilated her report card and was suspended for three years.[61] Irena's role model had been her father, who never refused medical aid to either Jew or gentile, and often treated those on whom society had turned its back. She recalled, "Once a female Jewish student friend of mine was beaten so severely that I attacked one of the assailants with my fists and spat at his feet, exclaiming, 'You bandit!'"[62]

What neither Irena nor the Jews of Poland, nor indeed all of Eastern Europe, could know was that their treatment at the hands of university officials was a mere shadow of the vileness that would soon descend upon the country. Under Hitler, the entire academic structure in Poland was obliterated, and as many of its college professors that could be found were murdered by the Nazis.

In 1931 at the age of twenty-one, Irena married Mieczysław Sendler. Unfortunately, the two soon discovered that they were incompatible; Irena moved home to live with her ailing mother, and her husband joined the army. When the Nazis invaded Poland in 1939, Sendler was captured and dispatched to a German prisoner of war camp where he spent the ensuing four years.

All her adult life, Irena had fought against the blatant anti-Semitism that had reared its ugly head in Poland, while Hitler's threats to the Jews left her incensed. Her escapades as a student fighting against such injustice forced Irena to forego her desire to teach—she was deemed undesirable. After petitioning a newly appointed official, she was granted the right to return to university and received her master's degree. In 1932, she became a social worker in the Mother and Child Aid Society, an offshoot of the Child Committee for Social Help. The organization provided legal and health-care assistance to the needy. It was her role to interview those who applied for assistance. When the offices closed in 1935 due to political pressure, Irena found employment with the Social Welfare Department. It was to become her greatest blessing as war engulfed Poland. It would provide contacts in an ever-broadening network that would help Irena achieve her goal—to rescue Jewish children from the hands of those men intent on murdering them.

On the night of November 9, 1938, and continuing into the following day, Germans and Austrians witnessed the implementation of a riot that would have political reverberations across Europe: *Kristallnacht*, or the Night of the Broken Glass. The attack was predicated on the shooting of a staff member at the German Embassy in Paris: A seventeen-year-old Jewish youth had supposedly retaliated for Nazi conduct toward his family in Germany. On October 27, 1938, the family of Herschel Grynszpan and more than 15,000 Jewish men, women, and children were loaded onto a train and summarily dumped at the Polish border to fend for themselves. It was a golden opportunity for Hitler's Minister of Propaganda, Joseph Goebbels, to take advantage of the situation and ignite the German population to take vengeance against all Jews. The memo from Heinrich Mueller, the final commander of the Gestapo, was quite explicit:

1. Actions against Jews, especially against their synagogues, will take place throughout the Reich shortly. They are not to be interfered with; however, liaison is to be effected with

the Ordnungspolizei [uniformed police] to ensure that looting and other significant excesses are suppressed.

2. So far as important archive material exists in synagogues this is to be secured by immediate measures.

3. Preparations are to be made for the arrest of about 20,000 to 30,000 Jews in the Reich. Above all, well-to-do Jews are to be selected. Detailed instructions will follow in the course of this night.

4. Should Jews in possession of weapons be encountered in the course of the action, the sharpest measures are to be taken.[63]

A second order was issued on the morning of November 10 by SS-Obergruppenführer Reinhard Heydrich that clarified some of the measures to be taken by members of the Third Reich:

a) Only such measures should be taken as will not endanger German life or property (i.e. synagogue burning only if there is no fire-danger to the surroundings).

b) Businesses and dwellings of Jews should only be destroyed, not plundered. The police are instructed to supervise this regulation and to arrest looters.

c) Special care is to be taken that in business streets non-Jewish businesses are absolutely secured against damage.[64]

Heydrich was well-known for his cruelty and brutality, not just toward the Jews but to anyone who had the misfortune to have been placed under his jurisdiction. His own apprentice defined Heydrich as having "a cruel, brave and cold intelligence" and that for him, "truth and goodness had no intrinsic meaning."[65]

The events of Kristallnacht prompted one particularly successful attempt to move Jewish children from the path of Hitler's advancing agenda to safety in England: *Kindertransport*. Groups in Germany, Poland, Czechoslovakia, and Austria began to urge Jewish parents to allow their children to be transported to England and take up residence with families there who were willing to care for them. The British government agreed—with the stipulation that homes must be found. In all, some 10,000 children escaped Hitler's ruthless plan before the lifeline was severed.

The Nazis launched World War II by breaching the Polish border on September 1, 1939. Polish leaders fled to Britain where a government-in-exile was formed. That move allowed them to command war efforts of the army and resistance fighters in Poland and in other countries. Immediately, conditions for Irena Sendler, and those who along with her pledged to save the lives of children, proved to be harsher and infinitely more difficult. The penalties for giving aid and comfort to Polish Jews were harsh, even deadly. Each time Irena or someone in her group offered even so much as a sip of water to those being persecuted by the Nazis, it could be punishable by death. There were instances under Nazi rule where entire villages were razed because their residents dared provide aid to a Jew.

A devout Catholic, Irena readily volunteered to help the Polish Socialist Party care for Jews who had been deprived of even basic necessities or had been forced into hiding. The Warsaw city government leaders had been forced to terminate the employment of all Jewish workers and were forbidden from giving them any assistance. The disenfranchisement of Polish Jews was devastating to children who, along with their families, had become homeless. Having to work in secret was grueling for Irena and others who had risen to the challenge, as discovery could mean death or imprisonment—the suspicious and the betrayer lurked at every turn. In addition to their work of secretly providing for the Jews, Irena and her crew were tasked with feeding German prisoners of war in a Warsaw hospital. She and her fellow social workers established a mandate of pairing the more affluent citizens with those who were poorer, and to share what food and medicine they might have available.

As the Nazis assumed power in Poland, new and egregious laws against the Jews were enacted. Among them were: being commandeered into forced labor, compelled to wear a yellow star on clothing, robbed of the cash in their bank accounts and allowed only $50.00 per week, controlled by a 9:00 p.m. to 5:00 a.m. curfew, forbidden to travel by train, and obliged to disclose an inventory of all worldly goods—clothing, furnishings, gems, anything of value. As the snare tightened, Jews were deprived of synagogue services and schooling for their children.

Irena and her cohorts stepped into the breech and began to provide forged identity papers that carried the names of deceased Poles in order to provide ration cards and other welfare. Besides providing aid to the Jews in Warsaw, Irena and her helpers also provided necessities for other refugees

displaced by the joint German/Soviet invasion of her homeland. Near the end of 1940, the Nazis had herded the Jewish
population of Warsaw into a small section of the city that
became known as the Warsaw Ghetto. The German press
never referred to the area as a Ghetto; it employed such
benign words as *sealed* or *sequestered* within the specified
compound—a place necessary for "sanitary reasons." The
occupied area confined over 400,000 Jews in a compound
approximately 1.3 square miles in size, a place whose walls
were built by Jews forced to erect their own prison. Tricking
the inhabitants into believing they would be allowed self-
rule within the Ghetto, the Nazis appointed a *Judenrat*, or
Jewish council. A definition of the practice from Humbolt
University describes the method used:

> Most often composed of former community
> leaders, the councils took on all the duties of
> a local government. Most importantly for the
> Germans, the councils acted as intermediaries
> to carry out their increasingly oppressive dic-
> tates, such as providing forced labor battalions
> for German war factories, and eventually even
> delivering Jews directly to the trains bound for
> the death camps.[66]

On November 16, 1940, the gates leading into the Ghetto were slammed shut, trapping inhabitants inside the nearly ten-foot-high brick and barbed-wire walls. Anyone daring to venture outside the walls could have been shot on sight.

In the eighteen months following, a multitude of Jews from villages outside Warsaw were also thrust inside the walled compound. It was a maniacal and diabolical means to ensure that the Jewish population of Poland was available for deportation to death camps without the effort or expense of hunting them down. With that many people confined in such a small place, disease and starvation were certain to follow. Typhus was especially rampant in the buildings where many were confined to one room.

Author Charles G. Roland relates:

> By 1941, the official ration provided 2613 calories per day for Germans in Poland (including the Volkdeutsch [German people]), 699 calories for Poles, and 184 calories for Jews in the ghetto. [Israel] Gutman [Warsaw Ghetto survivor] states rather naively that there was "little chance" of surviving on the official ration alone. Actually, there was not the slightest chance for Poles or Jews to survive on the official ration.[67]

It was into this morass of Jew-hatred that Irena Sendler walked in her white nurse's uniform complete with a yellow armband. It lent her a certain amount of anonymity as she was allowed to enter the Ghetto daily under the pretext of taking food, medicine, and clothing to its inhabitants. She donned several layers of clothing over her slim physique in order to secrete as much contraband as possible.

Irena had been appalled when hundreds of thousands of Polish Jews had been herded into the sealed-off sixteen-block area and was determined to help save as many as she possibly could. She was alarmed to learn that some 5,000 men, women, and children were starving to death or succumbing to disease inside the walled-off slum. Each month, thousands were driven from their homes to the *Umschlagplatz*—railroad station—with little more than one small suitcase of possessions before being deported to Treblinka or other death camps. They weren't aware that even those treasured belongings would be snatched from them before being herded into a cattle car and bound for annihilation. During its relatively short period of operation—slightly more than a year—a staggering 800,000 or more Poles died in Treblinka, more than 60,000 individuals weekly, more than any other concentration camp with the exception of Auschwitz. Only those selected for "death duty"—removing those who had been murdered shortly after clearing the train cars—lived longer than a couple of hours after arriving at Treblinka.

Appalled by the dire circumstances inside the Ghetto, Irena devised and implemented a plan to rescue as many children as she possibly could. With great apprehension, Jewish parents relinquished their children into Irena's care. It was not an easy task to persuade them that their children would be safer outside the restrictive confines of the Ghetto. To be left inside was sure death; only outside did they stand any chance to survive.

Irena used every means possible to smuggle the children out of their prison: ambulances, coffins, hidden among dead bodies being picked up for burial, in burlap bags, and in false bottoms of toolboxes. Escape routes passed through buildings adjoining the walls, and even a church. They entered one door as a Jew, and exited as a Catholic with new identity papers. Susan Brophy Down wrote in her book about Irena Sendler:

> Smuggling children required a vast network of volunteers to act as guides or house the infants once they were free. They brought children to the streetcar station where a friendly driver was on duty. He would sit the child in an empty car and then stop at an isolated spot once

outside the ghetto. One of Irena's co-workers, or "co-conspirators" as they called themselves, would be waiting to take the child to a safe home.[68]

Within the walls of the Ghetto, Irena had a Jewish friend, Ewa, who often supplied her with information about the gate guards—which she could safely slip by and which to fear. During one visit, Ewa alerted Irena of a new guard on the Leszno Gate who had earned the nickname "Frankenstein." Ewa warned, "He shoots people for the slightest provocation and sometimes at random. Yesterday, I was walking down Leszno and heard pistol shots . . . I watched from a doorway as this ordinary-looking German soldier walked alone down the center of Leszno Street shooting at Jews who cowered in doorways . . . . He stopped to reload his pistol then continued on his way, shooting."[69]

Dissatisfied with slow death by starvation, the Nazis began in 1942 to round up 6,000 people per day and take them from the Ghetto to the railway station. There, they were herded into cattle cars and transported to a death camp where gas chambers awaited them. When Irena's activities were curtailed by more stringent SS security, she became one of the first recruits active in Warsaw in the Żegota Polish anti-Holocaust resistance. Funds were funneled into the organization from Jewish groups in the United States and secretly dispersed to those hiding Jews. Irena later reported:

> Vast sums passed through my hands and it was a great relief to me when I could prove that the money reached the right place [orphanages, convents, families housing secret Jews].[70]

One of the many children Irena was able to snatch from the jaws of death in the Ghetto was Elzbieta (Bieta) Koppel. She was whisked from her parents' apartment when she was only about six months old. As her family prepared the baby girl for Irena to sneak from the compound, Bieta's mother secreted in the swaddling clothes a silver spoon inscribed with the baby's name and date of birth. Irena gave the baby a small sleeping draught to keep her quiet and then hid her in a carpenter's toolbox. With the help of a bricklayer to whom the unusual conveyance belonged, she managed to safely extract the little one from the Jewish sector.

Once outside the gates, baby Bieta was given the name Stefia Rumkowska. She was taken to live with the midwife who had delivered her with the admonition from Irena, "Her name is Bieta. When you love her and hold her, call her Bieta."[71] The little girl survived the Holocaust; both her Jewish parents died. When she reached adulthood, the only remembrance she had of her loving parents was the tiny silver spoon her foster mother had preserved in a small wooden box.

Irena's commitment was not confined just to helping rescue children from the Ghetto; she was also charged with checking on the ones already in hiding, finding clothing, food, and arranging for bogus identification cards for those liberated.

One of the men who helped provide false identities was Julian Grobelny; he was also one of the leaders of Żegota. Not only did he work with Irena in rescuing children from the Ghetto, he and his wife, Halina, transformed their home into a way station for fleeing Jews. He aided Irena with the necessary paperwork to hide the Jewish children in plain sight. He and Halina are among those honored by Yad Vashem as Righteous Among the Nations.

At one point, Irena conspired, not to sneak someone out of the Ghetto, but to guide someone into it. Jan Karski, a Polish man dressed in rags, slipped inside the walls to document the treatment of the occupants. He then donned the uniform of a Ukrainian soldier to capture images of Jews being beaten and robbed at the train station before being taken to concentration camps. After risking his life to be smuggled out of Poland to Spain, then Britain, and finally the United States, Karski was appalled when his pleas to save the Jews fell on deaf ears. He met first with Supreme Court Justice Felix Frankfurter who, though not convinced, took Karski to the White House to meet with President Franklin D. Roosevelt. Karski reported to the president:

> There is no exaggeration in the accounts of the plight of the Jews. Our underground authorities are absolutely sure that the Germans are out to exterminate the entire Jewish population of Europe. Reliable reports from our own informers give us the figure of 1,800,000 Jews already murdered in Poland up to the day when I left the country.[72]

Poet T. S. Eliot wrote, "Humankind cannot bear very much reality."[73] That was certainly true of Karski's attempts to alert world leaders of the horrors taking place in Nazi-held Poland.

Eleanor Roosevelt said this about the way her husband dealt with unpleasant things: "If something was unpleasant and he didn't want to know about it, he just ignored it. He always thought that if you ignored a thing long enough, it would settle itself."[74] Karski said of the Holocaust and its staggering loss of Jewish life, "This sin will haunt humanity to the end of time. It does haunt me. And I want it to be so."[75]

Irena's assistance to Karski paled in comparison to her determination to save the children. Long after the war, Irena recounted that she could still hear the sobs of parents as they lovingly placed their offspring in her care. In some instances, parents would ask her to return the following day only to find that they had been whisked away during the night to certain death. She carefully noted both the Jewish and Christian names of the children and buried the lists in jars in the backyard of a friend. The lists contained the names of 2,500 youngsters.

In January 1943, the Warsaw Ghetto Uprising halted Irena's work to rescue children. By January 18, 1943, more than 300,000 had been transported to death camps, all the while thinking they were being relocated to work camps. Until that time, the belief was steadfast that those taken from the Ghetto had been relocated to labor camps. When that was proved to be false and upon learning that those moved had instead been killed in large numbers, those inside the walled-off compound decided to fight for their lives.

T he Warsaw Ghetto revolutionaries who opted to
fight back against further deportation did so with
only a handful of pistols, gasoline bombs, knives, lengths
of pipe, and homemade hand grenades, supplemented by
whatever arms could be captured from Nazi troops sent into
the zone. The approximately 65,000 Jews who remained
were no match for the better-armed and larger troop con-
centrations fighting against them. Once the uprising had
been checked, they were deported to death camps and the
area was razed except for the infamous Pawiak Prison.

In 1943, the Nazis discovered Irena's actions and arrested
her at her mother's apartment. Irena watched in horror as
the Gestapo relentlessly searched for the names of those
who were employed in rescuing Jews and of those rescued.

When she heard the pounding on the door, Irena had quickly passed the list of children to a friend who tucked them into her armpit, where they remained undiscovered. The Gestapo found nothing—including the stacks of counterfeit ID cards and packets of cash Irena kept hidden under her bed.

The police, angered by the unsuccessful search, arrested Irena and took her to Gestapo headquarters—a fearsome place where detainees were subjected to brutal methods of questioning. On her way to Gestapo headquarters for interrogation, Irena discovered a list of names in her coat pocket—names of children and their foster families due for assistance. She successfully tore the paper into tiny pieces and dispersed them through the window of the vehicle in which she was riding. Although relentless in their attempts to extract information from her, breaking bones in her legs and feet during the interrogation, Irena withstood the cruel torment, her lips sealed and her spirit unbroken. Eventually she discovered that her informant was the owner of a laundry who, during the same kind of vicious and inhuman inquisition that Irena had undergone, gave up Irena's name and those of several other underground workers.

After some time at Gestapo headquarters, Irena was transferred to an even more terrifying location: Pawiak Prison. The building, erected in the 1800s and located inside the Warsaw Ghetto, was confiscated by the Nazis for use as a detention center. There, Irena joined a group of women required to launder the dirty underwear of the prisoners and guards alike. On one occasion, some of the guards, deciding that the women had scrubbed the underclothing too vigorously, marched into the laundry area, lined the washerwomen up, and callously shot every other prisoner. Women on either side of Irena were fatally wounded; she was left standing, wondering how she had cheated fate.

In January 1944, after having been incarcerated for three months, Irena's name was called. Thinking that her death was imminent, Irena was astonished to discover that she and a group of thirty other women were being transported to Gestapo headquarters. Once there, she was shown into a room where one of the Gestapo members led her to an exit and informed Irena that she was free to go. Żegota members had bribed the official to release her and supply her with documents showing that she had been executed. From that moment until Poland was freed from the Nazis, Irena Sendler remained in hiding . . . just like those children whom she had rescued from the Ghetto.

Rather than bask in the limelight as a hero, Irena wanted no accolades for her efforts. Instead, she said, "I could have done more. This regret will follow me to my death."[76] At the end of the war, Irena and her coconspirators dug up the jars from under an apple tree. In them were lists with all the names and locations of the children who had been saved from death at the hands of the Nazi SS. They were given to a fellow collaborator in the Żegota, Adolf Berman. He, along with his staff, determined that almost all the parents of the children had been murdered at Treblinka or had simply disappeared.

Finally in May 1945, Nazi Germany surrendered and the Russian Army marched into Poland. Rather than being liberated by their own Home Army, the Poles became subjects of yet another tyrannical dictator, Joseph Stalin. After liberating Warsaw, the Red Army marched on to Auschwitz, where a mere 7,000 captives had barely managed to survive their treatment at the hands of the Nazi jailers. Among them were children who had lived through some of the most horrible days imaginable and who needed intensive care and consideration. Irena and a group of nurses joined together to provide love and attention for the traumatized youngsters.

Irena and her husband, Mieczysław, divorced in 1947; they later remarried, but that marriage also failed. After parting yet again from Sendler, Irena married a young Jewish man, Stefan Zgrzembski, whom she had known at university. The couple had three children, Janina, Andrzej, and Adam. Rather than being seen as a heroine who risked her own life to save others, Irena was viewed by the Soviets as a threat and imprisoned for months. She was brutalized by the secret police—the *Urząd Bezpieczeństwa*—because of her connections to the Polish Home Army, and as a result, her son Andrzej was born prematurely and died after only eleven days.[77] She eventually adopted two foster children— Teresa and Irenka. Both had lost parents during the war.

Why did Irena feel so compelled to risk her life to help others? From the book *Life in a Jar: The Irena Sendler Project* come Irena's own words:

> My parents have taught me that if someone is drowning one always needs to/should give a helping hand/rescue them. During the war the entire Polish nation was drowning but the most tragically drowning were Jews. For that reason, helping those who were most oppressed was the need of my heart.[78]

When Nazi troops initially swooped down on Poland, 3.3 million Jews resided in the country. When the war ended in 1945, only about one-tenth of that number, 380,000, had survived Hitler's Final Solution.

In September 2015, Russian Ambassador Sergei Andreev

charged Poland with having been partly to blame for World War II by "blocking the creation of an anti-Nazi coalition [making it] co-responsible . . . "[79] Andreev defended the Soviet incursion into Poland and the overwhelming defeat of the Polish resistance fighters as necessary in order to establish a "friendly country at its borders."[80]

Government leaders in Warsaw responded with: "We regard this as a lack of respect for the memory of victims of NKVD (secret police) crimes, perpetrated on the orders of the highest Soviet authorities."[81]

Rather than providing succor to the decimated Poles, the Soviets under the despot Joseph Stalin continued the practice of sending Polish citizens off to camps in Siberia where bitter winters, starvation, and exhaustion claimed many. In far too many instances, as in the case of Irena Sendler, the Soviets used horrific methods of interrogation to extract information from them.

Following the Soviet invasion of Poland, Irena continued her job as a social worker until she determined she could no longer support the prevailing communist regime. Her resignation from the party brought threats of arrest, but she was saved by the wife of a party official whom Irena had hidden during the war. Irena was accused of supporting

Israel during the 1967 Arab-Israeli War and was stripped of her government job. Her love for children drove her into a teaching role and to volunteer work with the Polish chapter of the Red Cross.

In 1965, twenty years after the war ended, Yad Vashem Holocaust Museum in Jerusalem honored Irena Sendler with the title of Righteous Among the Nations. Among the many awards presented was one she most treasured: being made an honorary Israeli citizen in 1991.

According to the London-based weekly newspaper *The Economist*:

> It was not until 1983 that the Polish authorities allowed her to travel to Jerusalem, where a tree was planted in her honour at Yad Vashem. Many of the children she had saved sought her out: now elderly themselves, all grateful, but some still yearning for details of their forgotten parents. In 2003 she received Poland's highest honour, the order of the White Eagle. It came a little late.[82]

Following that award, Irena received a letter from Pope John Paul II, which read, in part:

Please accept my hearty congratulations and respect for your extraordinarily brave activities in the years of occupation, when—disregarding your own security—you were saving children from extermination, and rendering humanitarian assistance to human beings who needed spiritual and material aid.[83]

Irena also received the Jan Karski Award in 2003 "For Courage and Heart" from the American Center of Polish Culture in Washington, D.C. She was also presented with a humanitarian award from the Audrey Hepburn Foundation in 2009. One of her greatest "awards" was receiving correspondence from some of the children whose lives she had saved.

Irena's life and efforts to save as many children as possible birthed the *Life in a Jar Project*. Norm Conard, a history teacher in the bucolic community of Uniontown, Kansas, challenged three of his students to participate in a 1999 National History Day assignment based on the life of Irena Sendler, a little-known heroine of the Holocaust. The three young women—Megan Stewart and Elizabeth Cambers, both ninth graders, and high school junior Sabrina Coons—accepted the challenge and began working on the project. It ultimately led to several meetings with Irena in Poland and revealed her bravery to the world. The team, after winning several awards for their presentation, was finally able to perform *Life in a Jar* in Warsaw. There they met the Chief Rabbi of Poland Michael Schudrich, who said to them:

> This moment is the ultimate revenge on Hitler. Protestant kids, celebrating a Catholic rescuer of Jewish children from the Warsaw Ghetto, performing in a Jewish theater in Warsaw. And they are being filmed by German television.[84]

Irena Sendler died on May 12, 2008, at the age of ninety-eight.

CHIUNE SUGIHARA

"Do what is right because it is right; and leave it alone."

—CHIUNE SUGIHARA

1

J ewish refugees looking for a way of escape from Nazi savagery knew him simply as "Sempo," a much simpler pronunciation of his Japanese name, Chiune Sugihara. It was not his name for which he was honored in 1985 as one of the Righteous Among the Nations at Yad Vashem—the only Japanese citizen to have been chosen. No, it was his efforts to save as many Jews as possible from the clutches of Hitler's henchmen.

Chiune was born to Yatsu and Yoshimi Sugihara on New Year's Day in 1900 into a middle-class family, the second of six children. The young hero-to-be did well in his studies, graduating with top honors from elementary school but deliberately failing an entrance exam that would have set him on the course of becoming a physician. Instead, he chose a path that led him to a diplomatic career.

After being drafted by the Japanese Foreign Ministry and posted to China, Sugihara became skilled in Russian and Germanic languages. His diligent study of Russian affairs earned him the classification of "expert" in that field. He was dispatched to Harbin, China, where he converted from Buddhism to Orthodox Christianity, a move that some think may have solidified Sugihara's campaign to save Jews fleeing Hitler's madness. Father John Bakas, an Orthodox pastor in Los Angeles, credits a chance invitation to a ceremony honoring Sugihara for his own outreach in the City of Angels. After hearing of Sugihara's exploits from surviving family members, Bakas said:

> Here's a man who did not take the comfortable road, who reached out beyond himself and did something sacrificial in providing service to others at the expense of himself. Sugihara had a tremendous impact on how I perceive my ministry.[85]

While in Manchuria, Sugihara married a Russian woman, Klaudia Semionovna Apollonova, but the two later divorced before he returned to his homeland. He later married Yukiko

Kikuchi and fathered four sons: Hiroki, Chiaki, Haruki, and Nobuki.

The year 1939 brought changes, not only to the Sugihara family but also to the world at large. In March of that year, Germany wrested control of the area known as Memel from Lithuania even as Chiune and his family were sent to Kovno (Kaunas), Lithuania's temporary capital. In August of that year, Dr. Chaim Weizmann presided over the twenty-first World Zionist Congress in Geneva, Switzerland. As the war clouds gathered, Weizmann ended his remarks to those gathered with these words: "I have no prayer but this: that we will all meet again alive."[86] He could not have foreseen the disaster that awaited his people before the twenty-second World Zionist Congress met again in 1946, its delegates bowed under the horrific news that six million Jews had perished in the intervening years.

Also in 1939 Italy invaded Albania; Germany attacked Poland, officially launching World War II; and war was declared on Germany by the United Kingdom, New Zealand, Australia, France, and Canada. In September, the United States would declare its neutrality.

Following the end of World War I, Lithuania was an independent country—at least until the seizure of Memel by the Germans followed by the Russian invasion in 1940 and the subsequent annexation of the country. With total disregard for the nationals, Hitler and Stalin had signed a nonaggression treaty that became known as the Molotov–Ribbentrop Pact, which would remain unchanged until Hitler ordered the invasion of the Soviet Union on June 22, 1941.

The pact designating that there would be no hostility between the two nations also stipulated that Lithuania, Latvia, Finland, Romania, and Poland would be divided without regard for the wishes of the population. Less than two weeks after the Soviets marched into Poland the pact was modified by the German–Soviet Treaty of Friendship, Cooperation and Demarcation.[87] A greater section of Poland was allotted to Germany and Lithuania—with the exception of the territory on the left bank of the Scheschupe River, which was awarded to the Russians. A third agreement, the defense and mutual assistance pact, allowed the Soviets to establish bases in Estonia, Latvia, and Lithuania.

As the Germans moved across Poland and began to drive the Jews into Ghettos and deport them to so-called "work camps," the population of Lithuanian Jews burgeoned by an additional 100,000 or more. It was into this maelstrom that Chiune Sugihara was drawn and his determination to help those threatened by the Nazis was sparked.

Once in residence in Lithuania, Chiune discovered that the Jewish community had its own diverse and unique ethos, including its own characteristic Yiddish dialect. Before the tide of Nazism engulfed the country, Jews accounted for approximately 7 percent of the populace, a total of about 160,000 individuals.

In Kovno, Chiune's first order of business was to establish a consulate in the city that held a tactical location between the German tyrant Hitler and Soviet Union dictator Joseph Stalin. It was not an enviable position. Author Hillel Levine wrote of a letter Sugihara penned to historian Dr. Roman Korab-Zabryk:

> As future consul in Kovno, where there were no army detachments at all, I soon realized that my major task would be to provide the General Staff [of the Imperial Japanese Army] and not the Ministry, all information based on events and rumours regarding the Lithuanian-German occupied border regions . . . and preparations by the German armies to attack the USSR. We needed new eyes in Lithuania.[88]

Sugihara's information would become even more critical to the Japanese following the German invasion of Poland on September 1, 1939. It would send a wave of Jewish exiles across the border into Lithuania. Chiune had friends among the Jewish community in Lithuania, among them the Minkowitz family. One of the young sons, Moshe, told of a "kindly and dignified diplomat"[89] who frequently visited their home. Was it these calls that would ultimately influence Chiune to unselfishly give aid to the Jewish people trying to escape Nazi reprisals? The Japanese consul was frightened by the stories of the brutal Nazi attacks against the Jews in Poland.

Initially, Lithuanian Jews pursued ordinary activities, perhaps thinking they would be untouched by the atrocities being carried out in other parts of Europe. Conceivably, they didn't totally comprehend the full breadth of events outside their country. Eventually, the horror swooped down in June 15, 1940—not an invasion by Nazi panzer divisions, but via Soviet ground troops. The Lithuanian Jews were caught in the middle; there was no escape eastward where death camps awaited. Incongruously, the Soviets were prepared to allow Lithuanian Jews to travel through the Soviet Union in search of a safe haven. The only prerequisite was that special documents were needed to permit passage.

The dire situation required that Consul Sugihara make detailed and dangerous decisions regarding the destiny of multitudes of Jewish families. Would the Japanese diplomat react with compassion and formulate a workable plan for those in danger? Or would he simply pack up his family and move them to safety as quickly as possible? He and Jan Zwartendijk, the Dutch envoy, were the only two emissaries still in Kovno.

After careful study, some of the Polish refugees discovered two avenues of hope in the far-off Caribbean—Dutch Guiana (now Suriname) and the island of Curaçao. The consul from the Netherlands assured the terrified migrants that their passports would be valid for travel to the two colonies, and permits would be granted to them. There was only one obstruction: Japanese transit visas were mandatory while attempting to traverse the Soviet Union. Why? A portion of the trek would take them across Japanese territory.

Anguish driven by the advancement of Nazi and Russian troops drove the Polish Jews to desperate measures as Chiune and his family would soon discover. One July morning in the summer of 1940, they awoke to the sounds of a multitude of people lined up outside their home. All were seeking the all-important transit visas that would allow them to apply for vital Soviet exit visas—all that stood between them and the death camps. It was the only hope of freedom and deliverance available to the dispossessed Poles.

"Sempo" Sugihara was troubled by their life-or-death predicament and in a quandary as to how he could assist them. The first order of business was to contact the Japanese Foreign Ministry in Tokyo for permission to issue transit visas to thousands of people. These were required for their survival. He wired his superiors, who denied his request; a second wire received the same response; a third and final wire was answered with the following:

CONCERNING TRANSIT VISAS REQUESTED PREVIOUSLY STOP ADVISE ABSOLUTELY NOT TO BE ISSUED ANY TRAVELER NOT HOLDING FIRM END VISA WITH GUARANTEED DEPARTURE EX JAPAN STOP NO EXCEPTIONS STOP NO FURTHER INQUIRIES EXPECTED STOP (SIGNED) K TANAKA FOREIGN MINISTRY TOKYO[90]

Sugihara had been reared and educated as a strict Japanese traditionalist, and this final transmission from Tokyo placed him in quite a dilemma: Did he follow orders as he had been trained to do, or did he follow his conscience as a Christian? Disobedience could end his career as a diplomat, and even his ability to be employed by anyone. In the Japanese hierarchy, this would have serious ramifications, not only for him, but for his children and his extended family. His actions could even place his wife and children in danger. On the other hand, his disobedience to the Japanese edict could save the lives of thousands. What to do? He called his wife Yukiko and his children together and explained the situation to them. The decision was that ethics outpaced the other dangers. Sugihara said that all he could do was to "Do what is right because it is right; and leave it alone."[91]

Chiune and his wife bravely made the decision to issue transit visas to those waiting outside the consulate gates.

Hillel Levine wrote of those days and the long lines of people:

> It started almost politely, with a steady trickle of individuals making inquiries, and it ended with long lines of agitated people standing there day and night . . . with the desperation of those who knew this might be their last chance to get out. . . . the man now known as Lewis Salton told me one crisp autumn day in 1994, "I must have been one of the first to receive the Japanese transit visa. Sugihara received me very nicely. He offered me tea . . . . He sat at his desk and wrote the visa in longhand.[92]

Richard Salomon, a member of the board of the Illinois Holocaust Museum and Education Center, whose father was the recipient of Sugihara's visa number 299, said of the consul:

> Without him, many of the most accomplished minds of our world would not exist today. His legacy produced doctors, bankers, lawyers,

authors, politicians, even the first Orthodox Jewish Rhodes Scholar.[93]

Once Sugihara had made the decision to help the Jewish refugees, his labor was nonstop. Every moment was precious; every visa represented a life saved. Anxiety was palpable; despair and despondency profound. Levine wrote, "The most vulnerable, the most miserable had arrived on his doorstep, and he could not turn away his eyes."[94] The Sugiharas would have had to dispense as many as two hundred visas daily in order to rescue the 6,000 individuals who stood outside night and day until allowed entrance to the consulate. The initial line of one hundred became one thousand and ultimately six times that number of men, women, and children.

Sugihara had no idea how long he would have before he would be forced to halt his activities and leave Lithuania; therefore, the sense of desperation left little time for sleeping or eating. He and Yukiko issued transit visas almost nonstop for twenty-nine days in late July and through August in advance of the September 1, 1940, date to close the consulate in Kovno.

Sugihara packed up his family for a rail trip to Berlin, all the while continuing to issue transit visas as hurriedly as possible. Even aboard the train, the Japanese diplomat passed out visas through the train window to as many of those who waited as possible. He even bequeathed his official seal and a stack of visas to a refugee in an effort to further the rescue operation.

With visas clutched in hand, the fleeing refugees quickly made their way to Moscow by train with a secondary destination: that of the Trans-Siberian Railway in Vladivostok. The ultimate goal was Kobe in Japan from where they would be directed to Shanghai in China. It was a grueling journey, but one willingly undertaken in order to survive.

Once in Kobe, the Jews faced a different culture. Holocaust expert Dr. David Kranzler said of the influx of refugees:

> Every single one of those people was permitted into Japan. Some of them had to go back and forth from Vladivostok to Japan several times, but eventually they were permitted to enter Japan. The refugees averaged a stay in Japan of eight months, some over a year. And one cannot understand it without realizing the Japanese governmental policy.
>
> And believe me, they kept tabs on every

refugee. Every foreigner, in fact. The word for foreigner in Japan meant "spy." So Japan was not that open at that point; . . . they were not interested in foreigners coming in general. And yet, they permitted the Jews to stay there; they were even good to the Jews in Kobe.

[In Kobe], there were Japanese who gave of their food. Japanese who gave of their rations, because Jews are not used to the rice ration, gave of their wheat ration, bread rations to Jews . . . . Doctors gave free inoculations. It had nothing to do with the government . . . .

Sugihara did not go against his government's grain. But he was a humanitarian by providing them with the opportunity to go to Japan. What they did in Japan was beyond his power. But he wanted to give them an opportunity to leave Russia, to leave German and Russian territories.[95]

In 1941 Gestapo Lt. Col. Josef Meisinger, known as the "Butcher of Warsaw," attempted to persuade the Japanese to either eliminate or imprison the tens of thousands of Jews who had fled to Shanghai for safety. In their book, *The Fugu Plan: The Untold Story of the Japanese and the Jews During*

World War II, authors Marvin Tokayer and Mary Swartz wrote that the Nazi *Obersturmbannführer* Meisinger was more than willing to outline his plan. He related to the vice-consul, Mitsugi Shibata, in Shanghai:

> There are now in Shanghai, over seventeen thousand Jews who have chosen to leave the fatherland. In January of this year, the German government very wisely deprived these traitors of their citizenship. They are enemies of the German state and potential, if not already actual, saboteurs against you, our ally. For the good of our alliance, we strongly feel that the entire Jewish plague must be eradicated from Shanghai. You need not worry about the mechanics, we will handle all the details. You will merely reap the rewards of our labors: you, of course will inherit everything the Jews presently own or control.[96]

The Nazi's repugnant and nauseating suggestions included:

1. Stripping the Jewish refugees of all clothing, placing them on several old and useless freighters, towing the ships to sea and disabling them.

Once all aboard had perished, the ships could be torpedoed and sent to the bottom of the ocean.

2. Rounding up the refugees and making them slaves in the Japanese salt mines. Meisinger assured his audience that the Germans were well versed in getting the most work for the least amount of nourishment possible.

3. Confining the ill-fated Jews in a concentration camp on Tsungming, an island in the Yangtze River. There they would be "allowed" to volunteer for grotesque medical experiments—some of which the salivating Nazi described to the vice-consul and his associates.

Although Meisinger's suggestions were rejected by Shibata, the Japanese did confine many of the Jews who had been declared "stateless refugees" in a ghetto erected in the Hongkew quarter. Jews could only leave the quarter with special permission. While two thousand died of old age and disease, the inhabitants were not tortured; nor did they face other mistreatment as did the Jews confined in ghettos in Europe.

T housands of men, women, and children who had fled into Lithuania seeking asylum survived under the auspices of the Japanese governing body in Shanghai because of the actions of Chiune Sugihara. Following his stint in Lithuania, he was dispatched to Prague where he labored in 1941 and 1942. The situation in Lithuania disintegrated rapidly in June and July of 1941 as the Germans invaded and occupied the country. German *Einsatzgruppen* (mechanized killing detachments) began massacring the Jews in rural areas. Survivors were confined to ghettos in Vilna, Kovno, and several other towns and to labor camps. As it was in Warsaw, so it was in the ghettos of Lithuania where starvation, disease, and torture were routinely carried out against the Jewish residents. Of the 40,000 survivors of the roving killing groups, some 30,000 were sent to labor camps, extermination camps, and concentration camps. Three years later in 1944, when the Soviets reentered Lithuania, ninety percent of the Jews in that country had been murdered—one of the highest death tolls in all of Europe.

The lives of 6,000 had been secured thanks to Chiune Sugihara. He had been transferred to Bucharest where he, too, fell victim to the Soviet invasion in 1944 and was regrettably sent, along with his family, to a prison camp. There they remained for a year and a half. The Sugiharas were finally allowed to return to Japan in 1946. A year after his return, Chiune was forced to resign from his diplomatic career. Some speculated it was due to his noncompliance with the order not to issue visas to the Jewish refugees.

After his return home, Chiune lived a life of relative obscurity, working at various jobs to support his family—in one instance as a door-to-door salesman of light bulbs. It was a time of extreme poverty for the man who had risked his life to save so many. He also worked as a translator and interpreter before being offered a job in Moscow with a Japanese company. Sugihara was forced to leave his family in Japan, visiting them only a few times during his fifteen years in Russia. What he could not know was that many of those whom he had saved petitioned the Japanese government for information about the man who was their rescuer, all to no avail. Conversely, Chiune never spoke to others regarding his work among the Jews in Lithuania.

That all changed in 1968 when Joshua Nishri, a man who had emigrated to Palestine and had become an Israeli official, launched an effort to find the Japanese diplomat who had helped him and so many others survive. Not until then had Sugihara realized the numbers of those who had escaped the clutches of the Nazis and their Final Solution. The following year, his efforts were acclaimed by the Israeli government. When he arrived in Israel, he was met by another Sugihara survivor, Zerach Warhaftig, yet another official in the Israeli government. "Sempo" was deeply moved by the knowledge that many of the people who had stood in long lines outside the consulate in Kovno had made it to safety.

Chiune Sugihara, a virtual unknown in his own home-land, died in 1986, a year after being acclaimed one of the Righteous Among the Nations at Yad Vashem in Jerusalem. His neighbors were astounded when a sizeable delegation of Jews from many nations attended the funeral of their unassuming friend. The inhabitants of Yaotsu, his home-town, honored him with the Chiune Sugihara Memorial. In 1995, his wife, Yukiko, wrote *Visas for Life*, the story of her husband's exploits in Lithuania. That was followed in 1997 by the formation by his son Hiroki of the Visas for Life Foundation to continue the legacy of Chiune.

In 2007 the World Youth Leadership Network staged a concert at Carnegie Hall to honor Sugihara. Israeli concert performer and songwriter Zamira Chenn wrote "The Heart Remembers Still" in honor of the Japanese diplomat. The chorus echoes the heartfelt thanks of so many that had escaped because of Sugihara:

> It is all because of you my friend
>
> A stranger whose soul found the way
>
> To save my life and give me hope
>
> You are in heart night and day
>
> You are in heart to stay.[97]

THE TEN BOOM FAMILY:
CORRIE, CASPER, BETSIE

"LIFE IS BUT A WEAVING"
(THE TAPESTRY POEM)

"My life is but a weaving
Between my God and me.
I cannot choose the colors
He weaveth steadily.

Oft' times He weaveth sorrow;
And I in foolish pride
Forget He sees the upper
And I the underside.

Not 'til the loom is silent
And the shuttles cease to fly
Will God unroll the canvas
And reveal the reason why.

The dark threads are as needful
In the weaver's skillful hand
As the threads of gold and silver
In the pattern He has planned

He knows, He loves, He cares;
Nothing this truth can dim.
He gives the very best to those
Who leave the choice to Him." [98]

1

WAR! Tanks rolling into the town square. Bombs dropping like deadly, oversized hailstones from the skies. Choking pillars of smoke and dust rising in the air. The grating sound of soldiers' boots stomping through the streets. The staccato explosions of gunfire. Cries of terror and pain, and then an unsettling, eerie silence. These were events that happened in other countries—in Germany, for instance—but not in neutral Holland. At least that's what Cornelia Arnolda Johanna (Corrie) ten Boom thought in 1939.

When recording the Righteous Among the Nations in Yad Vashem the names of Corrie ten Boom, her sister Elizabeth "Betsie," and her father, Casper, certainly could not be omitted. Their heroism was too great, their sacrifice too noble.

The family's initial close encounter with Adolf Hitler's teachings was with Otto, a young German, who had come to Haarlem to study the art of watchmaking under Casper ten Boom. He proudly introduced himself as one of Hitler's Youth and embarked on a series of surreptitious attacks against Christoffels, an old watch mender in the ten Booms' shop.

It was Corrie's brother, Willem, who finally pinpointed the cause of Otto's rude and belligerent behavior. He explained, "It's very deliberate. It's because Christoffels is old. The old have no value to the State. They're also harder to train in the new ways of thinking. Germany is systematically teaching disrespect for old age."[99]

When Corrie's father protested that Otto had shown no animosity toward *him*, Willem continued, "You're different. You're the boss. That's another part of the system: Respect for authority. It is the old *and the weak* who are to be eliminated."[100]

Otto's behavior finally came to a head one morning as Christoffels staggered into the shop—coat torn and with scratches on his face. Although he said nothing about his injuries, Corrie noticed his missing hat and went in search of it. As Corrie ran down the street to retrieve the hat, she encountered Otto surrounded by a crowd of angry people.

He had been seen forcing Christoffels into the side of a building and grinding his face into the rough bricks.

Casper's attempts to reason with Otto were useless, and he was forced to send the young German home. The last the ten Booms saw of Otto was his look of glaring contempt as he strode down the street away from their home and shop.

On May 10, 1940, the people of Holland came face-to-face with the reality of war: Germany invaded their country, which had hoped to remain neutral. Earlier in the evening, the ten Boom family had gathered around Casper's prized radio to hear the Dutch prime minister address the country. He assured the people that there was nothing to fear. Casper was incensed by these comments. The prime minister's dire prediction: "It is wrong to give people hope when there is no hope. It is wrong to base faith upon wishes. There will be war. The Germans will attack, and we will fall."[101]

Shortly thereafter, Corrie was in bed asleep when the jarring sound of explosions rent the night. She bolted upright and grabbed her robe. Slipping her arms into the sleeves, she raced downstairs, paused outside her father's room, and hearing only the sounds of his whiffling snores, moved on to her older sister Betsie's room. Corrie felt her way across the bedroom to find Betsie, who was sitting upright in the darkness. The two sisters embraced and said in unison, "War."

They curled up in Betsie's bed and drifted back to sleep. That was when Corrie dreamed that she, Betsie, their father, brother Willem, and nephew Peter were being driven through the square in Haarlem in the back of a wagon. To her horror, they were unable to climb down from the dray that was carrying them farther and farther from their home. She jerked awake and told Betsie about the dream. Betsie reassured Corrie, "If God has shown us bad times ahead, it's enough for me that He knows about them. That's why He sometimes shows us things, you know—to tell us that this too is in His hands."[102]

Five days later, following one of Germany's most successful blitzkrieg campaigns, the news came that Holland had surrendered and Queen Wilhelmina had escaped to England where Dutch leaders and the queen established a government in exile. While resistance against the German invasion lasted for days, the battles claimed the lives of approximately 2,300 Dutch soldiers and over 3,000 civilians; some 7,000 were wounded.

During the months that followed, the Dutch people gradually became aware of the horrors of anti-Semitism. At first, it was negligible—a rock through a window or slurs painted like ugly slashes across synagogue walls and on the front doors of Jewish homes. Jews were increasingly denied service in restaurants, libraries, theaters, and other gathering places. Finally, six-pointed yellow stars were handed out that had to be worn prominently on clothing, each bearing the word *Jood* (Jew). Although not a Jew, Casper ten Boom obtained a star and proudly wore it on his coat. Then silently and ominously, Jews began to disappear, as if they had never existed.

On one of their walks, Corrie and her father saw Jews in the public square being loaded like so many cattle into the back of a truck—men, women, and children—all bearing the ignominious yellow star. Corrie wept for the people; Casper pitied the Germans, for, he said, they were "touching the apple of God's eye."

It was Corrie's nephew Kik, Willem's son, who was responsible for helping the Weils, the ten Booms' neighbors across the street, escape the Nazi threat, and who planted the thought in her mind of working with the underground. Once the seed was planted, God began to water it and cultivate it until, on May 10, 1942, the seedling burst forth into the light, and the lives of the ten Boom family were forever changed. (Kik died in Bergen-Belsen. He was incarcerated for having aided a downed American pilot.)

The edict had been handed down from Nazi headquarters that singing the Dutch national anthem "Wilhelmus" was *verboten* (forbidden). One Sunday Corrie, Betsie, and Casper were attending the service as usual at the Dutch Reformed Church in Velsen, a small town nearby. The German occupation had been responsible for one good thing in Holland: Churches were filled to overflowing with worshippers. Peter, another nephew, had been selected as church organist in a competition of forty entrants. He was in the organ loft, hidden from the crowd below. As the service concluded, the crowd emitted a unified gasp; Peter had pulled out all the stops on the huge organ and was playing the "Wilhelmus" at full volume.

Peter was clearly a hero to the burdened Dutch people, but Corrie worried that he might be arrested for his bold organ recital. For several days his safety seemed secure, but then Peter's little sister, Cocky, burst into the clock shop to inform everyone that Peter had been arrested and taken away to the federal prison in Amsterdam. For two months he would languish in a cold, dark, concrete cell at the prison before finally being released.

Two weeks later, the ten Boom family home became a way station on the underground railroad, which aided Jews in escaping the Nazis. Just before evening curfew a knock summoned Corrie to the alley door. There stood a heavily veiled woman. When the door opened, she stepped inside and identified herself as a Jew seeking asylum. Casper welcomed her and explained that all of God's children were welcome in his home. Two nights later, another furtive knock sounded at the side door. An elderly couple stood there, also seeking asylum.

The following day, Corrie traveled to seek Willem's advice. As he talked with Corrie about how to procure ration cards, she thought of a friend who worked in the Food Office. With the help of Fred Koornstra, Corrie was able to secure enough ration cards to feed the Jewish refugees who passed through the ten Boom home.

The secret room or "The Hiding Place," as it would later become known, was the brainchild of one of Europe's most respected architects, whom they knew only as Mr. Smit. (Many of the underground workers were labeled "Smit." This made it nearly impossible for other workers to identify and endanger these brave volunteers.) This elderly wisp of a man freely gave his time and energy to design and direct workmen who built a room so secure that the Gestapo never found it. A signal was devised to show that it was safe to enter the ten Boom home. This was an Alpina Watches sign that was hung in the dining room window.

Once the room was completed, "guests" rehearsed again and again getting into the hiding place quickly until they could vacate the lower floors to safety inside the compartment in less than two minutes. Corrie practiced stalling techniques to delay anyone who might come in search of the hidden Jews. One of their guests, Leendert, a schoolteacher, even installed an alarm system that would sound an early warning if unwanted visitors threatened.

Since the ten Boom home was near the center of Haarlem, Corrie worked diligently to secure other hiding places for the people who came for help. She enlisted farmers, owners of large homes, and others who wished to give aid to the tormented Jewish population. She amassed a group of about eighty people, some of whom were teenagers, willing to risk their lives to carry coded messages between Corrie and her contacts. One coded message read:

> We have a man's watch here that's giving us trouble. We can't find anyone to repair it. For one thing, the face is very old-fashioned.[103]

That was translated as "an elderly Jew whose facial features would give him away." This was a most difficult individual to place in a safe house. The ten Boom family took him in and afforded a haven for him.

One afternoon, Rolf, a local policeman who had provided aid to the ten Boom family, stopped at the clock shop. He had information that the Gestapo was going to raid a local safe house that night. Corrie summoned Jop, a seventeen-year-old volunteer, and asked him to deliver a message about the planned raid. Unfortunately for Jop, the Gestapo had already swooped down on the home and were lying in wait for the unsuspecting young man. He was quickly arrested and transported to the prison in Amsterdam. When Rolf returned with the news of Jop's arrest, members of the ten Boom family were convinced they should stop their underground activities, but they courageously refused to abandon their Jewish friends. The work had to continue.

Corrie had been in bed for two days with influenza when, on February 28, 1944, a man claiming to need help to rescue his wife from prison came to the clock shop and demanded to speak only to her. Corrie painfully rose from her bed, dressed, and went downstairs. The visitor pleaded for 600 guilders in order to bribe a policeman and secure his wife's release. She arranged for the money, sent the man on his way, and slowly climbed back up the stairs to her sickbed. Sometime later she heard the incessant buzzing of the alarm system.

Corrie supposed a drill was in progress—but that was soon followed by the realization that it was no drill. She heard the sound of boots tromping through the downstairs and heavy footfalls on the stairs below her room. She secured the trapdoor to the hiding place, set her "prison bag" in front of the panel, and dove back into her bed, feigning sleep.

The door to her room burst open and a tall, heavyset man demanded her name. "Cornelia ten Boom," she replied sleepily. The Gestapo leader, Kapteyn, demanded that she rise and dress. He casually asked, "So, where are you hiding the Jews?" Corrie denied any knowledge of Jews or an underground ring. He watched as Corrie pulled her clothes on over her pajamas, and with a regretful glance at her bag, which she had stuffed with necessities in case of capture, turned and walked out of the bedroom. She was prodded down the stairs and into the kitchen, only to find that a uniformed soldier stood there. In the front room, Corrie was pleased to see the Alpina Watches sign lying smashed on the floor. Anyone walking past the shop would know it was not safe to enter its doors.

Another of the Gestapo led Corrie into a separate room to be interrogated. Again and again she was asked to reveal the secret room. When she refused, she was struck repeatedly, but she still refused to answer, although she could taste the metallic tang of blood in her mouth. She cried, "Lord Jesus, help me." Her captor threatened to kill her if she spoke that name again, but he did stop the beating and eventually led her back to the room where her other family members were being held.

Corrie was roughly shoved inside, and Betsie was led from the room. Corrie dropped into a chair and heard sounds of wood splintering as cupboard doors were smashed in search of the suspected hiding place. One German was sifting through treasures that had been secreted in a corner cupboard on a lower floor. As the architect of the hidden room had predicted, it was the first place the Gestapo looked in their search for Jews. The destruction continued for another half hour, yet no one was found. When Betsie returned to the room, she was bleeding and bruised but had kept silent during the interrogation.

As the ten Booms were escorted from their home, their sanctuary, Corrie realized her earlier vision was about to become a reality: She and her family were being arrested, and they would eventually be transported to some undetermined place from which they could not escape. They were taken first to the local police station and placed in the care of their friend Rolf. For the remainder of the day, they were forced to sit on the cold, hard floor of a large room with thirty-five members of the underground family, along with partners who had gathered in the ten Boom home for their weekly prayer meeting.

Rolf entered the room, spoke briefly to Willem, and then bellowed that there were toilets available that could be used under escort. After he left the room, Willem whispered to

Corrie that this would be an opportunity for those inside to dispose of any papers they did not want to fall into the hands of the Gestapo.

Casper, the frail eighty-four-year-old patriarch of the ten Boom family, was arrested and dragged from his home to the police station. There, he was also forced to sit for hours on a cold stone floor. According to the Gestapo, he was guilty and worthy of death for one reason and one reason only: He was suspected of having helped Dutch Jews evade arrest and deportation to Adolf Hitler's concentration camps.

The group waited in agony, wondering if they were destined to be executed before the sun rose on another day. One by one, they were questioned and their fate determined—some were released, while others were sent back to the airless hallway to continue in fearful suspense. As darkness fell, the frightened and disheartened group gathered around Casper like children flock to a beloved grandfather. Not able to encircle them with his arms, he embraced them with his voice as he quoted words from the Psalms that had for so long been life and health to him: "Thou art my hiding place and my shield: I hope in thy word . . . . Hold thou me up, and I shall be safe" (Psalm 119:114, 117 KJV). His prayer was a benediction some would never again hear.

Finally an official shouted, "Casper ten Boom!" The old

man struggled to stand on his arthritic legs into which the cold from the floor had seeped, riddled with painful pinpricks from the lack of circulation. He stumbled toward the door and was hustled inside the interrogation room, where he was questioned again. Calmly and assuredly, peacefully and politely, the old grandfather painstakingly answered the questions barked at him. The interrogator leaned back in his chair and, in one last effort to seize control over the self-disciplined octogenarian, smiled charmingly. Like the offer Satan made to Christ in the desert, the Gestapo leader sat forward and said, "Old man, if you promise us you will not save any more Jews we will let you sleep in your own bed."

Smiling the smile of the redeemed, Casper responded, "I would consider it an honor to give my life for God's Chosen People." Casper ten Boom's dedication and determination to assist the Jews came as the result of his father, Willem, having taken up the banner passed to him by his great-grandfather, Gerrit ten Boom, a Christian Zionist. The ten Boom clock shop was begun in 1837. The family sought to emulate Christ's love by having an open door to anyone in need. The patriarch of the family attended a church service in 1844 during which he was inspired to begin a weekly prayer meeting to pray for the peace of Jerusalem (see Psalm 122:6).

Casper continued the meetings, where the family and

others gathered specifically in prayer for the Jewish people. The meetings ended on February 28, 1944, when Nazi soldiers came to the house to take the family away. He had come face-to-face with evil incarnate in the form of the Gestapo.

Corrie, her siblings, their father, and other prisoners were loaded into buses and taken to Scheveningen in The Hague, a town about twenty-four miles south of Haarlem. When they disembarked, one of the guards pointed at Corrie's father and yelled, "Did you have to arrest that old man?" Willem led his father up to the check-in desk. The head of the prison peered into Casper's eyes and said, "I'd like to send you home. I'll take your word that you won't cause any more trouble."

Those standing nearby clearly heard his reply, "If I go home today, tomorrow I will open my door again to any man in need who knocks." As the group was led to their individual cells, none knew it would be the last time they would see Casper ten Boom.

Corrie's first taste of prison was a narrow cell that she shared with four other women. When the matron determined that Corrie was quite ill, she was transported to the hospital. The doctor diagnosed her with pre-tuberculosis, hoping that she would be allowed to stay in the hospital.

It was not to be; Corrie was taken from the hospital and returned to the prison, but not before one of the nurses had slipped her a small packet containing soap, safety pins, and four individual booklets containing the Gospels.

Corrie gradually recovered from the influenza and began to wonder what had happened to the other people from Haarlem who had been transported to the prison. She scratched each name of her family members who had been arrested on the stone wall of her prison cell. On Hitler's birthday, she had the opportunity to seek information. While the wardens celebrated, the prisoners were able to shout back and forth to each other and gather yearned-for knowledge of loved ones. She learned that her sister Betsie was still at Scheveningen, that Willem had been set free, and that Nollie had been discharged almost a month before. Corrie then entered "released" by the names of her brother and sister. Casper ten Boom had died ten days after his incarceration, but it would be much later before Corrie learned of her father's death. When the information reached her, she scratched beside his name the word *Released*. On March 10, 1944, Casper ten Boom had died at The Hague Municipal Hospital.

Shortly after the celebration, the door to Corrie's cell cracked open and a package landed with a thump on the floor. She was overjoyed to discover that it was from Nollie. Inside, she found a light blue embroidered sweater. It was like being enfolded in the comfort of Nollie's distant arms. The package also contained cookies, vitamins, a needle and thread, and a bright red towel.

As Corrie wrapped the items back up in the brown parcel paper, she noticed a discrepancy in the return address. Carefully peeling back the stamp she found a joyous message: "All the watches in your closet are safe." Corrie rejoiced; all six of the Jews they had been hiding had safely escaped the secret room. This, no doubt, helped her through the following four long months in solitary confinement, in which her only contact was a tiny ant that had found its way into her cell. She was grateful to God for friendship with even one of His smallest creatures. She shared crumbs from her daily ration of bread with the minuscule insect.

Corrie knew that eventually she would face a hearing at the hands of a Gestapo interrogator. Finally, on a cool May morning, she was summoned from her tiny room. She was led through a labyrinth of halls and a courtyard sparkling with the drizzle of rain before entering one of the huts where the hearings were being held. As she awaited her fate, she prayed, "Lord Jesus, You were called to a hearing too. Show me what to do."

The inquisitor, Lieutenant Rahms, noticed that Corrie was shivering from the cold, so he built a fire in the stove. He drew a chair forward, motioned for Corrie to sit, and very gently began to question his prisoner. For the next hour he probed, feinted, and parried in a grim dance to gain Corrie's trust and glean information from his affection-starved detainee. He began, "I would like to help you, Miss ten Boom, but you must tell me everything."

Corrie was glad that among the drills practiced in her home in Haarlem was one of answering questions if captured by the Gestapo. Her training stood her in good stead. The officer questioned her about the ration cards and how they were obtained. She was relieved that she had no knowledge of how they had been stolen. When asked about her other activities Corrie launched into a description of her work with the girls' clubs and with the mentally disabled. The lieutenant seemingly had no idea why she found that so rewarding.

Rahms chided her for her waste of time with the disabled. Corrie responded, "God loves everyone, even the weak and feeble. The Bible says that God looks at things very differently from us." The officer abruptly ended the session and sent Corrie back to her cell. As she was being led through the corridors, she later wrote of how she was alerted to pay special attention to Cell 312:

> Betsie's back was to the corridor. I could see only the graceful up swept bun of her chestnut hair. The other women in the cell stared curiously into the corridor; but her head remained bent over something in her lap. But I had seen the home Betsie had made in Scheveningen. For unbelievably, against all logic, this cell was charming. My eyes seized only a few details as I inched reluctantly past. The straw pallets were rolled instead of piled in a heap, standing like little pillars along the walls, each with a lady's hat atop it. A headscarf had somehow been hung along the wall. The contents of several food packages were arranged on a small shelf; . . . Even the coats hanging on their hooks were part of the welcome of that room, each sleeve draped over the shoulder of the coat next to it like a row of dancing children—[104]

Betsie had brought order into the chaos that surrounded the incarcerated women, and hope into the hopelessness that engulfed them.

From that time forward, as long as Corrie was in Scheveningen, the lieutenant helped her as much as possible. He arranged for her to be allowed to see her family, using the pretext of the reading of Casper ten Boom's will. While they were all together, Willem slipped Corrie a small, compact Bible secreted in a pouch that she could wear around her neck.

Although the lieutenant could supply aid, he unfortunately did not have the authority to allow her and Betsie to return home. Nevertheless, Corrie spent time reading the precious Gospels that had been smuggled to her. She rejoiced that Jesus' death, though meant for evil, brought forgiveness to all who accepted His gift. She prayed that God would use her troubles to bring good to others.

3

I n June 1944, the prisoners languishing in their cells at Scheveningen were told to pack what belongings they had, and were then lined up and marched to a train awaiting them at the station. As she stood in line to board, Corrie saw Betsie down the platform. Suffering from pernicious anemia from childhood, Betsie had been denied medication. Corrie saw at once how very ill she had become, and she wriggled her way through the throng to reach her sister. They embraced with the joy of knowing that they were together, at least for the moment.

The train chugged down the line toward the Vught labor camp in the south of Holland. The prisoners were assigned to barracks and forced to work long, hard hours. Corrie was dispatched to the building in which Phillips radios were made for German aircraft. She did her work in the Phillips factory with great diligence. Day after day she made as many mistakes as she dared while assembling the radios.

Life in the camp was exceedingly hard, and executions among the male prisoners were the order of the day. Yet Corrie and Betsie survived. Betsie taught Bible classes to those who gathered around each night. Eventually, a faint hope blossomed as word seeped through the camp that the Allies had invaded Europe. Unfounded rumors that the Allied forces were nearing Holland swirled through the prison like leaves flying in an autumn wind. Sounds of explosions filled the air, but they were later confirmed to be the work of Germans destroying bridges and railroad lines.

Late one evening, the loudspeaker in the men's camp blared out name after name, and then just as quickly fell silent—as if the life had been squeezed from it. A similar sense of foreboding settled over the women's camp, when suddenly the twilight was filled with the sound of volley after volley of gunfire. When the guns were finally silenced, more than seven hundred captives lay silent on the gruesome killing field.

The next morning the women were once again commanded to gather their belongings and report for roll call in a field outside the camp. As noon approached, the women were ordered to line up and were then marched to a railroad siding. Betsie clung to Corrie's arm, wheezing and gasping for each breath. Corrie slipped an arm around her and half carried her precious sister the final quarter mile to their destination. As the two sisters glanced around, they could see perhaps a thousand weary, hungry, thirsty, bedraggled women standing in single file along the railroad track.

Corrie looked around for the train that was to take them to their next destination but saw only what she described as "small, high-wheeled European boxcars" stretching out of sight in both directions. Soldiers marched down the line of women, stopping at each car to throw open the sliding door. Horrified, Corrie realized that they were to be herded into the small boxcars like so many cattle. Each car, which might comfortably have held only thirty or forty, was soon packed with eighty or more women. Those in the car with Corrie and Betsie developed a plan that would at least allow them to sit on the floor. With little food or water and no toilet facilities, the car soon reeked of human waste.

For three days and nights the train slowly made its way across the border from Holland into Germany. Finally the lurching locomotive screeched to a halt and the doors were thrown open. The women scrambled out into the sunlight and were at last able to drink their fill of water. They were lined up again and then marched through the countryside to the crest of a hill, from where they could see their destination: Ravensbruck. Its reputation had reached Holland long before Corrie and Betsie were incarcerated. It was infamous as an extermination camp for female prisoners.

For the first two days in the compound, surrounded by grey concrete walls intersected by gun towers, the women were forced to stay in the open. Rain poured down on them, turning the ground into a quagmire of mud. When it wasn't raining, the sun beat down mercilessly and there was nothing to shade the desperate women. Finally they were processed, forced to disrobe, prodded through showers, and issued thin dresses and worn shoes.

Corrie wondered how she would be able to secure Betsie's much-needed sweater and prevent the confiscation of her beloved Bible. Then she saw an opportunity to hide them behind a bench in the latrine area. She prayed that her subterfuge would not be discovered as she and Betsie later made their way through two searches. At last they exited the building, with Betsie's sweater tied around Corrie's waist and the Bible dangling between her shoulder blades beneath her dress. As soon as she safely could, Corrie gave the sweater to Betsie, who put it on under her dress so that it could not be seen by the guards.

The two sisters were then crammed into a barracks designed to hold 400 people. Now it was home to over 1,400 women forced to sleep on rickety platform beds swarming with fleas. Yet, in this desperate room, Betsie and Corrie retrieved their beloved Bible from its hiding place and proceeded to teach the gospel of Jesus Christ to these starving women. Betsie would read in Dutch, translate into German, and the words would flow back through the crowd in French, Polish, Russian, or Czech, coming full circle back to Dutch.

The indignity of the regular Friday searches revealed a dynamic truth about Christ's sacrifice that neither Corrie nor Betsie had ever conceived. As they stood naked and shivering before the leering eyes of the German guards, a passage from the Bible literally came alive for Corrie. She realized that Jesus, too, had been stripped of His clothing. Corrie later wrote:

> I had not known—I had not thought . . . The paintings, the carved crucifixes showed at least a scrap of cloth. But this, I suddenly knew, was the respect and reverence of the artist. But, oh, at the time itself, on that other Friday morning—there had been no reverence. No more than I saw in the faces around us now. I leaned

toward Betsie, ahead of me in line. Her shoulder blades stood out sharp and thin beneath her blue-mottled skin. "Betsie, they took His clothes, too."[105]

A Catholic theologian, Monsignor John M. Oesterreicher wrote of the forced nakedness of the Nazi prisoners in terms of self-worth:

> The forced nakedness of the prisoners was an attempt to divest them of their dignity as persons. Clothes not only protect and adorn the body, they also bespeak the spirit of man, his sense of beauty, his style, his respect for himself, his reverence for others. In short, clothes mark a man as a civilized being. When the victims were compelled to undress, they were robbed, therefore, of their part in civilization. They were thrown into a mass of like men, all drained of initiative, and the last flicker of resistance was snuffed out.[106]

Each morning, Corrie, Betsie, and the other women were rousted out of bed for roll call at 4:30 by the sound of riding whips striking the side of the building. Conditions inside were so deplorable, so filled with the sharp odor of unwashed bodies, strangling dust, crawling lice, and swarms of fleas, that the guards refused to go inside. Everyone had to be outside quickly and ready for work. If even one person was missing, all the women were forced to stand stick straight for hours while all were counted again and again.

C orrie and Betsie were assigned to work in the nearby Siemens factory. Their job: pushing a cart laden with heavy metal plates to a railroad siding and then unloading it. Their eleven-hour days were broken only by a meager lunch of thin soup and a boiled potato. Corrie and Betsie felt blessed, for those who did lighter work received no lunch at all.

As the desperate days mounted, Corrie found that she was more often forced to mete out her hoard of liquid vitamins she had managed to hide for Betsie. The bottle had been given to her before she left Scheveningen. Corrie was stunned when she realized that though she often shared the precious drops with as many as twenty-five women in a day, the contents never ran dry. She was reminded of the woman in the Old Testament, the widow of Zarephath, whose cruise of oil held a perpetual supply as long as there was need of it—all because she willingly shared all that she had with the prophet Elijah.

One day one of the nurses from the infirmary, a young Dutch woman, smuggled a bottle of vitamins to Corrie. She rejoiced to be able to refill her small bottle. God's provision was truly confirmed that night as she held her bottle upside down to drain the last drop. No matter how long she held it or how many times she tapped the bottom, the bottle refused to give up another single drop. As God provided the new, the old ran dry.

When prisoners became ill with a fever of more than 104 degrees Fahrenheit, they were taken to the camp hospital, but no treatment was given them even there. When the hospital grew too full to receive more patients, the weakest and sickest were placed in carts and taken to the ovens that dominated the center of the camp. The ten Boom sisters had truly reached Hell on Earth, and yet they continued to praise God for His care. No matter where Betsie found herself, she talked about Jesus to those nearby—standing in line at the dispensary, performing the backbreaking work assigned to her, waiting for her daily ration of bread—she spoke of her Lord and His desire to come into their lives.

Corrie later wrote of Betsie's and her ministry to the women in their barracks:

> A single meeting might include a recital of the Magnificat in Latin by a group of Roman Catholics, a whispered hymn by some Lutherans, and a sotto-voce chant by Eastern Orthodox women. At last either Betsie or I would open the Bible. Because only the Hollanders could understand the Dutch text, we would translate aloud in German. And then we would hear the life-giving words passed back along the aisles in French, Polish, Russian, Czech, and back into Dutch. These were little previews of heaven, these evening meetings beneath the light bulb.[107]

Corrie recalled how, as the women were laboring in the prison yard one day, Betsie was maliciously lashed by one of the guards. She refused to allow Corrie to give in to hatred, praying instead for her captors as much as she prayed for the captives surrounding her. As the ruthlessness increased, Betsie's faith seemed to grow exponentially. She seemed to move even closer to God, her suffering but a small thing in light of His sacrifice.

When she returned to the barracks, Betsie told Corrie of her longing to have a place where people wounded in body and spirit could come to be healed after the war. One night as the sisters lay side by side in the barracks, Betsie told Corrie more of her dream:

> It's such a beautiful house, Corrie! The floors are all inlaid wood, with statues set in the walls and a broad staircase sweeping down. And gardens! Gardens all around it where they can plant flowers. It will do them such good, Corrie, to care for flowers.[108]

Betsie's desire was to tell people of the goodness of God—of what a good and wonderful Father He is. She wanted to teach people that hatred and bitterness must be left behind. Like the apostle Paul, she yearned to forget "those things which are behind," and to reach "forward to those things which are ahead," and to "press toward the goal for the prize of the upward call of God in Christ Jesus" (Philippians 3:13–14 NKJV).

Later, Betsie revealed another vision to Corrie, one of a concentration camp. It had been cheerfully painted, flowers ringed its periphery, barbed wire was gone, and guards no longer paraded on its walls. It would house the people who had been vilely treated by Hitler's minions, or whose lives had been infiltrated by his evil. They would once again be taught to be loving and kind to those around them.

As the fall days shortened into winter's icy blast, Betsie became more and more ill. Before long her body began to fail and she was coughing up blood. She was not a candidate for hospitalization, as her temperature lingered at 102 degrees. Then one fateful night, it finally topped the 104 mark, and she was placed in the hospital. Corrie accompanied her as, with the unexpected help of one of the more brutal matrons, Betsie was taken from the barracks on a stretcher to the hospital. The night was heavy with sleet as Corrie walked beside her sister and tried to shield her from the icy onslaught. When Corrie returned to the dormitory, her dorm mates assaulted her with inquiries about her beloved sister.

Daily, Corrie sneaked over to the hospital to stand outside the window where she could see her sister. One fateful day she peered through the dirty glass and saw only an empty bed. She slumped as she trudged away from her place of vigil. Suddenly she heard, "Corrie!" She turned to see the young Dutch nurse, Mien, who had provided so much assistance to those prisoners in the barracks. She grabbed Corrie by the arm and dragged her back to the hospital. "You have to see this," Mien pleaded. As the two neared the place where Betsie's body lay, Corrie looked at her face and there was the Betsie of Haarlem. Gone were the lines of grief and hunger and disease. Betsie's face was one of repose, of peace, of radiance. At last she was home with her earthly father and her heavenly Father. Corrie took time over the next days to share Betsie's miraculous transformation with her dorm mates.

One morning at roll call Corrie heard, "Prisoner ten Boom report after roll call." She thought surely her time must be up. Would she be punished for sharing the gospel with others, or would she be shot? When she reported, she learned that she was to be released, but her hopes were dashed when she was ordered to report to the hospital for swelling in her feet. Corrie spent weeks hospitalized before she was declared well enough to leave. Finally her medical release was stamped.

In a shed near the front gate, she was given new clothes: undergarments, a wool skirt and silky blouse, sturdy shoes, a hat, and a coat. When she was handed a document that stated she had never been ill while in Ravensbruck, she gladly signed the form. She was overjoyed when her watch—a gift from her father— was returned, along with her mother's ring and a few Dutch guilders.

At last the heavy gates swung open and a group of

about a dozen inmates was marched through them. Corrie thought there must have been some mistake. Surely she was being taken to the Siemens plant to work or to a local munitions factory. But instead of turning right toward their work places, the group was directed left toward the train station.

Finally, after a grueling trip with many delays, Corrie reached Berlin on New Year's Day 1945. She and Betsie had both been liberated—Corrie to life anew and Betsie to life everlasting.

After Corrie crossed the border into Holland, she spent almost two weeks in a local hospital, recovering her strength from the cruel ordeal she had suffered. One night she was smuggled to Willem's home onboard a truck ferrying food and supplies. Sometime later, Corrie learned that she had been released from Ravensbruck by a clerical error; a week after her departure all the women her age in the camp were brutally slaughtered.

As soon as she was fit enough, Corrie began to share her story with others. When the war ended, she related Betsie's vision of a place of asylum with a lady, Mrs. Bierens de Haan, whose son had been miraculously returned from a German prison camp. She was so grateful for his return that she gave Corrie her home for Betsie's legacy. It was a place of peace and comfort where the wounded and scarred—physically and emotionally—could receive succor.

The story of Corrie's wartime experiences began to reach other countries. She was invited to speak in America, England, and many other nations. The most difficult place for her to go was to Germany, a land scarred by bombs and hatred. Its cities were heaps of rubble, and the citizens' minds and hearts were covered with the ashes of despair. Corrie knew that the Lord would "give them beauty for ashes, the oil of joy for mourning, [and] the garment of praise for the spirit of heaviness" (see Isaiah 61:3) if only the German citizens would surrender their lives to the living Lord.

In Corrie's own words, she described an encounter with one of the former guards from Ravensbruck:

> At a church service in Munich I saw the former SS man who had stood guard outside the shower room . . . He came up to me and said, "How grateful I am for your message, Fraulein. To think that He has washed my sins away!" He thrust his hand out to shake mine . . . I who had so often preached the need to forgive kept my hand at my side . . . I breathed a silent

prayer: Jesus, I cannot forgive him. Give me Your forgiveness. As I took his hand the most incredible thing happened . . . a current seemed to pass from me to him, while into my heart sprang a love for this stranger that almost over-whelmed me.[109]

A Christian organization in Germany providing relief to the German people asked Corrie to help run a camp for those whose lives had been wrecked under Hitler's malevolent rule. When she arrived, she was stunned to see living proof of her sister's vision spread out before her. It was the abandoned concentration camp of which Betsie had dreamed. Its dull, dreary barracks were surrounded by bales of corroded barbed wire. Upon its paths of coal ash had trodden the feet of prisoners destined for death. Inside the empty barracks were row upon row of cots. If they could talk, oh, what tales of bravery, courage, despair, faith, or hopelessness they would be able to relate!

Corrie began to share Betsie's plan with her companions. They would need brightly painted window boxes filled with flowers, paint the color of sunshine for the inside walls, and the color of trees on the outside. And, of course, the horrid barbed wire must go before anyone would be allowed onto the grounds. This place must be a place of refuge, peace, and renewal.

Corrie was further able to relate the Good News of God's faithfulness and love to those around her. For over thirty years, she traveled from country to country calling herself "a tramp for the Lord." She shared Betsie's story and her own experiences at the hands of their captors while spreading the gospel. She traveled to communist countries that others avoided as being too risky, and she wrote numerous books. Perhaps the most famous was *The Hiding Place*, which later became the movie produced by Dr. Billy Graham. As her fame spread, so did her ministry.

Cornelia ten Boom suffered a debilitating stroke in 1978, robbing her of the ability to communicate. She died on her birthday, April 15, 1983, at the age of ninety-one. Certainly, no Jew who was saved because of the sacrifice of her family, all the Jewish women with whom she and Betsie shared the gospel and ministered to in the prison and concentration camp, and even the Germans who received the Lord due to their testimony will ever forget Corrie, Betsie, or their family.

Corrie's favorite psalm was the ninety-first: "He that dwelleth in the secret place of the most High shall abide under the shadow of the Almighty. I will say of the Lord, He

is my refuge and my fortress: my God; in him will I trust."
Indeed, she did abide under His shadow and trust Him!

In 1968, Corrie was honored as Righteous Among the
Nations at Yad Vashem in Jerusalem. In 2008, she was joined
by her father, Casper, and sister Betsie. It was my great honor
to have been invited to participate in the induction ceremony
along with Israeli Ambassador to the Netherlands Harry
Kney-Tal.

RAOUL WALLENBERG

"I will never be able to go back to Sweden without knowing inside myself that I'd done all a man could do to save as many Jews as possible."

—RAOUL WALLENBERG

R aoul Wallenberg came into the world as a member of one of the most moneyed and politically respected families in Sweden, where the name was tantamount to entrepreneurship, influence, and service. He was born in a town near Stockholm in 1912 to Raoul Oscar and Maria Sofia Wising Wallenberg. His father succumbed to cancer three months before the birth of his son, and his maternal grandfather died of pneumonia just three months after Raoul's birth. When he was six years old, his mother married Swedish physicist Guy von Dardel, with whom she had a son and daughter.

Raoul's prearranged naval career was out of the question when his stepfather discovered that Raoul was color-blind. When asked to prepare an art assignment, young Wallenberg proudly presented to Guy a landscape with green horses and red grass.

At the tender age of eleven, Raoul traveled alone from Stockholm to Istanbul, Turkey, to visit his ambassador grandfather. Unbeknownst to the young man, he was under the constant eyes of several well-paid railroad conductors. His trips abroad uncovered an easy grasp of foreign languages; he quickly learned English, German, and French—a talent that would be of immeasurable help later in life.

Raoul attended high school and a short military service in Sweden, and was then sent to Paris to study. In 1931, he traveled to the United States where he studied architecture at the University of Michigan in Ann Arbor. Although his family's wealth was legendary, Raoul was required to work at odd jobs when not hitchhiking around the country and into Canada and Mexico during school holidays.

In a letter to his grandfather, Gustav Wallenberg, the young voyager wrote:

> When you travel like a hobo, everything's different. You have to be on the alert the whole time. You're in close contact with new people every day. Hitchhiking gives you training in diplomacy and tact.[110]

Raoul traveled like a hobo to the Chicago World's Fair in 1933 in the back of a very teeth-jarring truck. At the time, little notice had been taken of the fact that Adolf Hitler had engineered an election to head the Third Reich. At that moment, the young college student—and the world—were oblivious to the monstrous hate that was about to seize Europe and spread its tentacles around the globe.

At the World's Fair, Raoul was engaged to do various jobs in the Swedish pavilion—souvenir selling, equipment hauling, light changing, window washing—all for the princely sum of three dollars per day. At the conclusion of his sojourn in Chicago, he again took to the road to get back to the campus in Ann Arbor. Standing on the highway waiting for a driver to stop, Raoul was picked up by four men, one of whom held a pistol. The young man was robbed of his summer earnings before being thrown from the car. Raoul landed in a ditch, his bag coming to rest atop him. In a letter home, he wrote of how calm and collected he was throughout the entire ordeal. Author Kati Marton shared Wallenberg's observations of what he had learned from that event:

> But he had learned something about himself,
> his own reactions and those of others when

confronted with the calm face of self-assurance.
It was a useful lesson.[111]

Little did Raoul realize how his demeanor would serve
him in the years ahead, when a sense of calm could mean
the difference between life and death. He had become a
"passionate student of the human psyche."[112]

After having been awarded his degree in 1935,
Wallenberg returned to Sweden. It was there that he met
Professor Ingemar Hedenius, a leading philosopher, and
revealed to him his partly Jewish lineage. He bragged to
the professor, "A person like me, who is both a Wallenberg
and half-Jewish, can never be defeated."[113]

During his absence Hitler's control had escalated; his
main target: the Jews. In 1935, the Nuremberg Laws were
enacted:

At the annual party rally held in Nuremberg . . . the Nazis announced new laws which
institutionalized many of the racial theories
prevalent in Nazi ideology. The laws excluded
German Jews from Reich citizenship and pro-
hibited them from marrying or having sexual
relations with persons of "German or related

blood." Ancillary ordinances to the laws disenfranchised Jews and deprived them of most political rights.

The Nuremberg Laws, as they became known, did not define a "Jew" as someone with particular religious beliefs. Instead, anyone who had three or four Jewish grandparents was defined as a Jew, regardless of whether that individual identified himself or herself as a Jew or belonged to the Jewish religious community. Many Germans who had not practiced Judaism for years found themselves caught in the grip of Nazi terror. Even people with Jewish grandparents who had converted to Christianity were defined as Jews.[114]

This heinous invasion into Jewish life would overshadow Wallenberg's future work in ways he did not comprehend.

Months after his return home, his grandfather Gustav arranged for Raoul to travel to Cape Town, South Africa, in the employ of a Swedish construction materials company. Shortly before setting sail, Raoul entered and took second place in a design contest. The challenge was to create a plan to refurbish an abandoned site along the river near the Royal

Palace in Stockholm. If you were to walk that path today, the layout of the park near the wharf is very reminiscent of that laid out by Wallenberg.

In a subsequent letter to a friend, Gustav Wallenberg wrote of Raoul:

> First and foremost, I wanted to make a man of him, to give him a chance to see the world and through mixing with foreigners give him what most Swedes lack: an international outlook. . . . Raoul is a man. He has seen much of the globe and has come into contact with people of all kinds.[115]

In South Africa under his uncle Jacob's tutelage, Raoul soon discovered he was not cut out to be a banker. He felt there was too much negativity, too many times when clients had to be denied access to much-needed funds.

Wallenberg's excursion to South Africa was followed in 1936 by a brief stint in the Holland Bank in Haifa, Israel. It was there that he caught a glimpse of what the Nuremberg Laws were doing to the Jewish population of Europe. He saw daily signs that once wealthy and esteemed merchants, bankers, and entrepreneurs were now but ragged beggars on the streets of the Israeli town. Some had made their way to Palestine in hopes of finding asylum; but he also read the agonizing accounts of other Jewish refugees who perished in the waters of the Mediterranean in unseaworthy ships that could find no safe harbor. Raoul heard from the residents in his meager lodgings of the horrifying stories:

> . . . how they had gradually been stripped of all rights and turned into non-people, allowed to exist only at the grace of the Reich. It was Wallenberg's first exposure to the irrational and poisonous germ of anti-Semitism . . . . The impression this humbled segment of humanity made on him was to be permanent.[116]

In the spring of 1937, Gustav Wallenberg died, once again leaving Raoul without a father figure in his life, and without a sponsor or prospects. His godfather, Jacob Wallenberg, eventually secured a position for Raoul in the import-export industry in Stockholm. The business—Central European Trading Company—was owned by a Hungarian Jew, Kálmán Lauer.

As events of the mid- to late-1930s led ominously toward a Second World War, the Nazis under Hitler had already been searching for a "final solution" to what they considered the Jewish problem.

On January 20, 1942, Hitler's architects of death met at the beautiful Wannsee Villa located in a serene lakeside suburb of Berlin. Their stated objective was to find a "Final Solution to the Jewish Question."

Presiding over the conference was SS-Lieutenant General Reinhard Heydrich, chief of the Security Police and Security Service. As the meeting began, Heydrich was determined that none should doubt his superiority or his authority, which was not limited by geographical borders. He briefed those in the room on measures that had already been taken against the Jews in an attempt to eradicate them from both the German culture and homeland.

In attendance were fourteen high-ranking German military and government leaders, among them Adolf Eichmann. Over a 90-minute luncheon, fifteen men changed the world forever. Initially, steps had been implemented to allow German Jews to immigrate to whatever countries would accept them, but the move proved to be too slow for the Führer and the Reich. Now the men gathered to implement Hitler's new—and final—solution. Heydrich provided a list of the number of Jews in each country; a total of eleven million Jews were to be involved. In his zeal he determined:

In large, single-sex labor columns, Jews fit to work will work their way eastward constructing roads. Doubtless the large majority will be eliminated by natural causes. Any final remnant that survives will doubtless consist of the most resistant elements. They will have to be dealt with appropriately, because otherwise, by natural selection, they would form the germ cell of a new Jewish revival.[117]

Translation: All must die.

After years of this continuous rhetoric, it took an hour-and-a-half—a mere ninety minutes—for Hitler's henchmen to determine the fate of six million Jews. During that period, roughly the time it would take to drive from Jerusalem to Tel Aviv during peak traffic, the Holocaust became a heinous reality.

According to the minutes of the meeting, Jews were to be purged, beginning in Germany, Bohemia, and Moravia. After that, they were to be expunged from all of Europe, east to west. Many questions arose as to how to identify those considered Jews. The issue was not resolved during the Wannsee meeting.

Of course, this was not the beginning of the extermination of the Jewish people. Many of the Nazi elite in attendance had already participated in mass murders since the summer of 1941. Even before the gathering at Wannsee, more than a half million Jews had been executed behind army lines. The question was how to attain the goal of *total* extermination in areas outside the battle zone. A more efficient way needed to be found to eliminate larger numbers. No, the meeting was not called to determine how to begin the process but rather to spell out how the "final solution" would be achieved.

While the Wannsee Conference was held to determine how to exterminate even more Jews, a vastly different conference held on the beautiful island of Bermuda in 1943 would determine the fate of Jewish refugees. Many in both Great Britain and the United States were clamoring for the Allies to rescue as many Jews as possible from the horrors of the Holocaust. Diplomats on both sides of the Atlantic worked to arrange a date for a meeting, which became known as the Anglo-America Conference on Refugees (the Bermuda Conference). An agreement was reached, and the symposium was set for April 19–30, 1943.

Harold Willis Dodds, president of Princeton, was selected

to lead the US delegation, and Richard Law, the British parliamentary undersecretary of state for foreign affairs, represented Britain. Chaim Weizmann, a leading proponent for the resettlement of Jews in Palestine, petitioned those assembled to allow more refugees to seek asylum in the Holy Land. When the conference drew to a close nothing of substance had been settled that would have saved some of the six million Jews from extermination.

A writer for the London *Observer* penned:

> Here are the leisurely beach hotels of the Atlantic luxury island, where well-dressed gentlemen assemble to assure each other in the best Geneva fashion that really nothing much can be done.... The opening speeches of the conference have been widely noted in this country, and noted with dismay and anger. We have been told that this problem is beyond the resources of Britain and America combined . . . If Britain and America cannot help, who can? . . . What is so terrible about these speeches is not only their utter insensitiveness to human suffering. It is the implied readiness of the two greatest powers

on earth to humiliate themselves, to declare themselves bankrupt and impotent, in order to evade the slight discomfort of charity.[118]

These two events would, in essence, lay the foundation for Raoul Wallenberg's rescue efforts in Hungary. The Battle of Stalingrad would open the door for Hitler to wreak havoc on Hungarian Jews. The conflict lasted for approximately seven months and was considered by the Russians to be a coup of great magnitude. It halted the advance of German troops into the Soviet Union and changed the course of the war in favor of the Allied armies. Unfortunately, it was also one of the most devastating confrontations of the entire war with nearly two million casualties, both civilian and military.[119]

After the Russians had won the battle of Stalingrad, the Hungarian government made the decision to attempt to negotiate a separate peace treaty with the Russians. The Führer had been angry before he called Hungarian leader Miklós Horthy; after their conversation, he was *infuriated* because Horthy had refused to accede to the demand that Hungary continue to side with Germany. Hitler ordered the German army to invade the ally in March of 1944. That was followed almost immediately by the deportation of the country's Jews.

O n January 22, 1944, after the atrocities perpetrated upon the Jews in Europe had finally become public knowledge, President Franklin D. Roosevelt issued an executive order establishing the War Refugee Board (WRB). The board was given the directive to work for the "immediate rescue and relief of the Jews of Europe and other victims of enemy persecution."[120] It was almost certainly too little, and far too late.

Meanwhile, Raoul Wallenberg's studies in the United States and his very prominent name led to his nomination by Iver Olsen, a Swedish member of the WRB, as a candidate for a mission to Hungary, despite his age and lack of political experience. Wallenberg was called to a meeting with Olsen while leading a group of Swedish National Guard volunteers through war exercises in the countryside. He had developed marksmanship abilities and stamina during those outdoor maneuvers even as his fate was being decided in Stockholm. Following his acceptance, Wallenberg was given special rank as a Swedish diplomat tasked with doing everything possible to rescue Jews. Wallenberg is said to have prefaced his departure with a memo to his superiors in the Swedish Ministry for Foreign Affairs. The letter, according to sources, stated:

> He was determined not to let himself be buried in diplomatic protocol and bureaucracy. He requested full authority to deal with anyone he wanted, without first clearing the matter with the Swedish ambassador in Budapest. He also wanted the right to use diplomatic couriers outside of normal channels. His memo was so unusual that the matter was referred all the way up to Prime Minister Per Albin Hansson, who consulted with King Gustav V before informing Wallenberg that his conditions had been accepted.[121]

In a move designed to clear the way for Wallenberg to travel to Hungary, the Americans involved in his appointment arranged his leave of absence from the Swiss National Guard.

The fate of the Jews in Hungary had, for all intent, been sealed when the Nazi occupation began in March 1944. By the time Wallenberg set foot on Hungarian soil in July, Adolf Eichmann had already orchestrated the removal of more than 400,000 Jewish men, women, and children. They were inhumanely plucked from outside Budapest and sent to Auschwitz and Birkenau in the southern reaches of Poland. The number dispatched was the equivalent of 148 trainloads of Jews—whose fate was an almost sure death sentence. As Jews in Budapest learned of the fate of their countrymen, desperation grew and the number that waited outside the legations of neutral countries grew exponentially. Temporary passports were issued to Jews who had even the most remote ties to those states.

The Swedish Embassy dispensed 700 passports—a miniscule number compared to the enormity of the threat to the approximately 200,000 Jews remaining in Budapest. Those holding these precious papers were deemed to be Swedish citizens and accorded the same courtesies as natural-born Swedes.

While Wallenberg was making his way to Budapest, the Roosevelt administration began a series of radio broadcasts designed to alert the Jews in Hungary. In the message delivered by President Roosevelt, he warned those who might help the Nazis that full retribution for war crimes would be instigated by the U.S. and pledged his support for the Jews until they were freed from Hitler's tyranny.[122]

Even as the airwaves were filled with promises of rescue, Jews began to disappear from Hungarian towns and villages. Those in Budapest were convinced they would be next. Desperate for help, they asked for provisional identity passes from the embassies of neutral nations. The passes were often issued to Jews who had any sort of ties to those particular countries.

King Gustav V of Sweden had directed a plea to the Hungarian head of state, Miklós Horthy, appealing to him to halt the expulsion of Jews, and Horthy courageously complied. He said in a letter to the king that he had taken all possible measures to abide by the monarch's request. In a move that baffled all involved, the Germans halted the extraditions of all Jews. They inexplicably went so far as to return a trainload of Jewish men, women, and children to Budapest. Historians believe that was the direct result of Germany's losses and impending defeat at the hands of the Western Allies. Perhaps Nazi leader Heinrich Himmler saw the handwriting on the wall and determined it was time to perfect his skill at negotiating. As a result, Himmler left Eichmann swinging in the wind in Hungary.

Before Wallenberg's arrival in Budapest, the head of the *Croix-Rouge suédoise* (Swedish Red Cross), Valdemar Langlet, had rented edifices and hung signs identifying them as a library or a research facility. They would be used as hiding places for Hungarian Jews.

Perhaps Wallenberg's lack of diplomatic training was actually an advantage, for it allowed him to employ other, more eccentric options—from bribes to coercion. His machinations were successful and caught the eye of other diplomatic colleagues. His first assignment was the drafting of a new passport motif that would assist the Jews in their efforts to escape the Nazis. The documents were impressive, with colors of blue and yellow to mimic Sweden's flag with the Three Crowns coat of arms centered and affixed with appropriate hallmarks and signatures. Wallenberg's initial print run was confined to 1,500 passports, but he managed to finagle another 1,000 from Hungarian authorities. Ultimately, through the use of futile guarantees and subtle bullying, Wallenberg's quota was raised to 4,500 passports that were actually worth no more than the paper on which they had been printed.

Wallenberg then took up the cause of the Jews in the capital city. During the last six months of 1944, he and Swedish diplomat Per Anger managed to issue counterfeit identification papers and passports to approximately 100,000 Jewish people. The papers identified the holder as a Swedish subject waiting to be repatriated. The sham worked. The recipients were spared deportation, thus saving them from the Nazi machine.

With his own funds, Wallenberg leased thirty-two buildings in Budapest. He announced that they were safeguarded by diplomatic immunity and displayed signs to reinforce that statement. Outside, he hung huge, ostentatious flags of Sweden. Before the war ended, he had housed as many as ten thousand Jews in the buildings.

Desperate to find an ally among prominent Nazi officers in Budapest—or at least one that could be easily enticed with bribery—Wallenberg happened upon Paul Szalai, a police officer and powerful member of Arrow Cross, the Hungarian Nazi Party. The party had come to prominence following the downfall of Horthy's government and his deportation. Szalai became Wallenberg's pawn in the government—someone who would look the other way or provide aid when necessary.

The Arrow Cross Party was as effective as the Nazis in its determination to annihilate the Jews of Hungary, and one of its first acts was to invalidate Wallenberg's "protective passports." The move would have crushed a lesser man, but in his determination to defend the Jewish people, Raoul made friends with Baroness Elizabeth "Liesel" Kemény. As the wife of the foreign minister, she had the ear of the man who could once again approve the permits.

The upsurge of the Arrow Cross Party also opened the door for the return of Adolf Eichmann, the architect of Hitler's Final Solution. Under Horthy, he had been stifled, now he had free reign. One of Eichmann's first measures was to institute forced death marches of sizeable numbers of Jews between Budapest and Austria. So brutal were the conditions those men and women were forced to endure that it brought censure from even the Nazi troops ordered to accompany the captives. Thousands upon thousands of bedraggled Jews in makeshift rows staggered across the landscape—literally chased by none other than Raoul Wallenberg. He cajoled, he enticed, he persuaded those in charge to identify and release those who carried Swedish "protection passes."

According to author David Metzler:

> When Eichmann's killers transported the Jews in full trains, Wallenberg intensified his rescue efforts. He even climbed the train

wagons, stood on the tracks, ran along the wagon roofs, and stuck bunches of protective passes down to the people inside. At times, German soldiers were ordered to open fire but were so impressed by Wallenberg's courage that they deliberately aimed too high. Wallenberg could jump down unharmed and demand that the Jews with passes leave the train together with him.[123]

By threatening to have him charged with war crimes at the end of the conflict, Wallenberg was eventually able to somehow persuade Eichmann to abandon a last push to round up any remaining Jews in Budapest. Having discovered a plot by Eichmann to annihilate an entire Jewish ghetto, Wallenberg went directly to the commander of the German army in Hungary, General Gerhard Schmidhuber, and actually intimidated him into halting the proposed massacre—by threatening to have him hanged for war crimes after the Russians entered the country. Within days the Russians, as expected, marched into Budapest and, depending on the source quoted, between 70,000 and 100,000 lives were saved due to the bravery of Wallenberg.

3

When Soviet troops advanced into the out-skirts of Budapest on January 13, 1945, they were met by the sight of a lone man standing outside a rather imposing building. Draped just above his head was a large Swedish flag. In Russian, the man introduced himself as Raoul Wallenberg, the Swedish chargé d'affaires for those areas of the country that had been freed by the Soviets. He petitioned for authorization to visit the Soviets' military command center in Debrecen, outside Budapest. It was his desire to explain in detail a plan he had devised to provide aid to surviving Hungarian Jews.

As he and his chauffeur left the city, Raoul halted long enough to say good-bye to those known as "Wallenberg's

Jews" who occupied the buildings the Swede had leased. He confided to his friend Dr. Ernö Petö that his fate was uncertain: Would he become a guest of their liberators, or a prisoner? As he walked away, Wallenberg is quoted as having said: "I don't know if they're protecting me or watching me. I'm not sure if I'm their guest or their prisoner."[124] The Swedish diplomat was never seen again.

Why? Once he had met the Soviets in Debrecen, were they so distrustful of a man who had devoted years to rescuing condemned Jews that they refused to heed him? Was he taken for an American or, God forbid, a German spy? Were the Soviets too besotted with their military success in Hungary to pay any attention to the likes of a bleeding heart such as Raoul Wallenberg?

It is thought that he died in captivity in 1947. On March 8, 1945, a Hungarian radio broadcast made by Soviet-regulated media announced that Raoul Wallenberg had been assassinated on the way to Debrecen. The culprits: the Hungarian Arrow Cross or Nazi sympathizers. Was it a genuine clue or a staged cover-up?

Seeking definitive information, appeals were made to the Soviets, who responded in 1957 that after extensive inquiries new information had been uncovered. The evidence of his last days was in the form of a handwritten document which read that "the prisoner Wallenberg, who is known to you, died last night in his cell."[125] It had officially been signed by a man named A. L. Smoltsov, head of the Lubyanka prison infirmary, and directed to the Soviet minister of state security.

In 1981, President Ronald Reagan bequeathed upon Raoul Wallenberg an honorary US citizenship, one shared at that time by only one other foreigner—Winston Churchill. In 1985, Wallenberg was designated an honorary Canadian citizen, and in 1986, an honorary citizen of Israel.

At Yad Vashem in Jerusalem, there is a street named Avenue of the Righteous. The lanes are lined with trees that bear the names of Righteous Gentiles—one dedicated in 1966 stands in honor of Raoul Wallenberg. Attorney Gideon Hausner, former chairman of Yad Vashem and prosecutor of Adolf Eichmann, said of Wallenberg:

> Here is a man who had the choice of remaining in secure, neutral Sweden when Nazism was ruling Europe. Instead, he left this haven and went to what was then one of the most perilous places in Europe. And for what? To save Jews.

He won this battle and I feel that in this age when there is so little to believe in—so very little on which our young people can pin their hopes and ideals—he is a person to show the world, which knows so little about him. That is why I believe the story of Raoul Wallenberg should be told . . . [126]

The daughter of former U.S. Representative Tom Lantos, whose life was saved by Wallenberg, delivered an impassioned speech at the UN Holocaust remembrance events in January 2008. She paid this tribute to Wallenberg:

> During the Nazi occupation, this heroic young diplomat left behind the comfort and safety of Stockholm to rescue his fellow human beings in the hell that was wartime Budapest. He had little in common with them: he was a Lutheran, they were Jewish; he was a Swede, they were Hungarians. And yet with inspired courage and creativity he saved the lives of tens of thousands of men, women and children by placing them under the protection of the Swedish crown.[127]

Most recently, Raoul Wallenberg was honored in the newly established Friends of Zion Heritage Center and Museum in Jerusalem. His remarkable story is now preserved for yet another generation of men and women who vow, "Never again!"

THE LIGHTS IN THE
DARKNESS IN LE
CHAMBON-SUR-LIGNON

*"Look hard for ways to make little
moves against destructiveness."*

—ANDRÉ TROCMÉ

1

Le Chambon-sur-Lignon is a French commune or municipality in south central France on the Lignon du Velay, a tributary of the Loire River. During World War II, its inhabitants were predominantly Huguenots, a protestant group that embraced the teachings of John Calvin. In the sixteenth century, they were subjected to harsh persecution and ultimately scattered around the globe.

The descendants of those Huguenots were no strangers to tyranny, and were well-suited as protectors of the men, women, and children on the run from Nazi oppression. As Adolf Hitler's troops marched through France toward the English Channel, the residents of Le Chambon-sur-Lignon willingly reached out with loving hearts to Jewish refugees seeking asylum.

In May 1940, Hitler's 9th Panzer Division launched a blitzkrieg (violent surprise war) against the Netherlands and Belgium. The French, certain that the mountainous Ardennes region was impregnable to Nazi tanks, were stunned when seven armored divisions reached the Meuse River in mid-May. When the dust and smoke of battle settled, France had lost 390,000 soldiers, while Germany had lost less than ten percent of that number. The stunning rout of French troops forced Premier Paul Reynaud and his government in Paris to abandon its headquarters for Tours, a city located between Orléans and the Atlantic Ocean.

When Nazi troops marched into the heart of Paris on June 14, Reynaud, certain that Hitler could not be stopped, recommended that the government relocate to French-owned property in North Africa. Vice-Premier Henri-Philippe Petain decried the solution and demanded that the French seek to sign a truce with the German tyrant. The resolution was put to a vote, which Reynaud lost. Petain was appointed premier and immediately began to negotiate with the Nazis.

According to historian John Simkin, the terms of the armistice were as follows:

France [was divided] into occupied and unoccupied zones, with a rigid demarcation line
between the two. The Germans would directly
control three-fifths of the country, an area that
included northern and western France and the
entire Atlantic coast. The remaining section
of the country would be administered by the
French government at Vichy under . . . Petain.

Other provisions of the armistice included
the surrender of all Jews living in France to
the Germans. The French Army was disbanded
except for a force of 100,000 men to maintain
domestic order. The 1.5 million French soldiers
captured by the Germans were to remain prisoners of war. The French government also
agreed to stop members of its armed forces from
leaving the country and instructed its citizens
not to fight against the Germans. Finally, France
had to pay the occupation costs of the German
troops.[128]

Petain, with his faulty reasoning, pinpointed what he
thought was the cause of Hitler's occupation of France,

"The chief cause of the moral collapse of the French Army was alcohol, and this is the worst of France's four major problems."[129] The people of France would soon learn that their problems far exceeded Petain's pitiful predictions.

Within months, restrictions were enacted against the Jews of France. Autumn 1940 arrived and with it the enactment of a census to identify Jewish inhabitants, giving the Vichy government a head start on deportation procedures. In the areas immediately surrounding central Paris, including its suburbs, approximately 150,000 Jews, oblivious to the implications, willingly registered with the aid of French gendarmes. With names, addresses, and pertinent information readily available, the Jews were fish in a barrel—easy to identify, locate, and arrest. Adolf Eichmann, head of Jewish affairs and "evacuation," ordered the information gathered by the Paris police be delivered to Theodor Dannecker, chief of the Gestapo in France.

A Statute on Jews was disseminated by Petain's government on October 3, 1940. It effectively established Jews as second-class citizens and launched apartheid (racial division) in France. The abhorrent yellow stars became mandatory, Jews were banned "from the administration, the armed forces, entertainment, arts, media, and certain professional roles (teachers, lawyers, doctors of medicine, etc.)."[130]

In his book *Let Innocent Blood Be Shed*, author Philip
Hallie wrote:

> Vichy did not intend to *destroy* the Jews, as
> the Nazis intended to do, only to eliminate them
> from the body politic of France, and Petain
> himself refused to let the Germans require that
> Jews in the Southern [Unoccupied] Zone wear
> the yellow star that identified them for hatred,
> ridicule, and capture in the streets. But Vichy
> singled them out for contempt, deprivation, and
> imprisonment, and thereby helped the Nazis
> greatly in their program to destroy the Jews
> of Europe.
>
> The National Revolution had as one of its
> overarching ideals a smoothly running machine
> purified of all recalcitrant grains of sand, free
> of all "dangerous anarchists," ... Among these
> forces for anarchy that would disturb the
> smoothly oiled functioning of this machine were
> the Jews. The unlimited authority of Petain
> and the seamless unity of France demanded ...
> the sequestration of the Jews, economically,
> politically, culturally, and physically in the

brutalizing concentration camps that extended across the body of France.[131]

Cardinal Gerlier, the archbishop of Lyons, later observed the movement that was labeled "The National Revolution" only served to reduce France to a "new order . . . built on violence and hatred."[132]

On October 24, 1940, Henri-Philippe Petain met Adolf Hitler in Montoire-sur-le-Loir, an isolated village approximately 129 kilometers (80 miles) south of Paris. There, the head of the Vichy government and the bully of Berlin would agree to an alliance and embark on a handshake, the photograph of which would be the perfect propaganda tool for Hitler. Six days later, Petain would announce via a radio broadcast to his French constituents, "I enter today on the path of collaboration" (*"J'entre aujourd'hui dans la voie de la collaboration"*). [133] This speech, cited during Petain's trial for treason in 1945, was pertinent in leading to his conviction and his sentence of life in prison.

After the signing of the armistice, the Nazis moved into Paris. Hitler gleefully toured the city, accompanied by his favorite architect, Albert Speer. During a whirlwind, three-hour tour, the Führer and his entourage visited the Paris Opera House, the Champs Elysees, the Trocadero across the

Seine from the Eiffel Tower, and the Basilica Sacré-Coeur (Basilica of the Sacred Heart) on Monmartre. Afterward, Hitler commented, "It was the dream of my life to be permitted to see Paris. I cannot say how happy I am to have that dream fulfilled today."[134]

Later, in his memoir, *Inside the Third Reich,* Speer commented:

> That same evening he received me once more in the small room in the peasant house. He was sitting alone at table. Without more ado he declared: "Draw up a decree in my name ordering full-scale resumption of work on the Berlin buildings . . . . Wasn't Paris beautiful? But Berlin must be made far more beautiful. In the past I often considered whether we would not have to destroy Paris," he continued with great calm, as if he were talking about the most natural thing in the world. "But when we are finished in Berlin, Paris will only be a shadow. So why should we destroy it?" With that, I was dismissed.[135]

Even as Hitler split France into two regions—unoccupied under Petain and occupied under the Führer—cataclysmic changes were about to be felt in both zones, and not just for Jews. The divided country was no longer a republic. Petain had seized the power to terminate elected officials and had, by the stroke of a pen, issued executive orders overriding constitutional precepts. The Vichy leader had adopted Hitler's "leadership principle." It was a simplistic hypothesis:

> Rudolf Hess probably best summarised the Führer Principle when he said in a public speech: "Hitler is Germany and Germany is Hitler. Whatever he does is necessary. Whatever he does is successful. Clearly the Führer has divine blessing."[136]

It was that concept that lent gravitas to Petain's power grab. His picture replaced those of other symbols of France; he acquired solidarity through aversion—to Jews, Communists, Freemasons, the English. It was to this "new" France that the people of Le Chambon-sur-Lignon and the Vivarais Plateau were introduced in October 1940.

The advent of more stringent laws governing Jews led the inhabitants of Le Chambon-sur-Lignon and those of other small towns in the vicinity to band together. They determined to provide a refuge for what would eventually number approximately 5,000 Jews fleeing for their lives from the Nazis.

Perhaps the people who lived in the villages were influenced by their history, thus hardening their determination to resist the Vichy government and their Nazi occupiers. Those Huguenot descendants knew the chronicle surrounding their own persecution by French Catholics during the sixteenth, seventeenth, and eighteenth centuries. It only made them more determined to not see others suffer the same prejudice, deprivation, and carnage. They believed that according to the Holy Scripture Jews were God's chosen people. When the time came to lead the escaping Jews from a certain death in France to the "Promised Land"—the Swiss border—they followed a path that had once been trod by their own tormented Huguenot ancestors.

After the Vichy government came to power, a pastor and dedicated peacemaker, André Trocmé of the Reformed Church of France, his wife, Magda, and his part-time assistant, Pastor Edouard Theis, were determined to launch a peaceful revolt against the new administration. Trocmé was particularly disturbed by the blatant anti-Semitism that he observed within the ranks of the Petain government. Journalist Michael Curtis wrote of "French Christian Decency":

> It was Trocmé who, after France surrendered to Nazi Germany, said it was the responsibility of Christians to "resist the violence that will be brought to bear on their consciences through

the weapons of the spirit." It was also he who protested in a sermon on August 16, 1942 against the roundup of 13,000 Jews in Paris by saying that "the Christian Church must kneel down and ask God to forgive its present failings and cowardice."[137]

When cooperation with Petain's Vichy government was expected and compliance demanded, the residents of the Vivarais Plateau declined to ring area church bells in tribute. Ordered to adopt a Fascist salute—raised arms stiff, palms down—Trocmé considered the decree an opening for nonviolent resistance. He had seen the masses in Germany saluting Adolf Hitler in the same manner, and knew it was symbolic of abandoning those people deemed unworthy by both Petain and the Führer.

The Trocmés and Theis became the main facilitators for rescuing those fleeing Nazi persecution, but were joined by others including Catholics, members of the Society of Friends (Quakers), Protestants from Switzerland, Evangelicals, and even some with no religious ties. The effort to safeguard those being sought by Eichmann in his madness to implement his so-called "final solution" commenced in the winter of 1940.

Trocmé knew the reputation the Quakers had enjoyed in France and Germany following World War I. He knew that the conscientious objectors cared only for the suffering, and that they were allowed access to prisoners by both the Germans and the Vichy government. With that knowledge, Trocmé called upon a group of Quakers in Marseilles and asked for supplies to aid some 30,000 Jews being held in captivity in the south of France. The inmates were bereft of food, clothing, and medical aid, all of which the Quakers were desperately trying to provide.

Burns Chalmers, the American head of the group, advised Trocmé that he might, indeed, be of assistance to those incarcerated—by negotiating their freedom. There was only one drawback: No refuge was available for them. The pastor from the village of Le Chambon assured Chalmers that its residents would willingly accept and provide for the evacuees.

Philip Hallie wrote of the Quaker and his affinity with Trocmé's village:

> Chalmers had seen in Le Chambon the cru-
> cial condition for effective action on behalf of
> the children, the weakest of the weak: security,
> freedom, within a given ethical space where

goodness could overcome evil without hindrance from the outside world. A village surrounded by rugged mountains and on a high plateau that was difficult to reach.[138]

When a knock was heard on their door, day or night, rain or shine, the Trocmé's opened it and welcomed those standing outside. Magda was a whirlwind of charisma and organization, a woman who "knew how to find food when there was no food and just which door to knock on to find room and welcome for those her own overburdened household could not accommodate."[139] When she realized just how great the need was, she immediately began to mobilize the townspeople and persuade them to reach out selflessly to those in need. As a result of the courage of the inhabitants in the towns and villages surrounding Le Chambon, more than 5,000 Jews were spared Hitler's revenge.

With the assistance from many in surrounding hamlets and villages, Trocmé was able to create a rare refuge in Vichy France. He and the members of his church were extremely valuable in establishing ways to conceal and care for Jews released from the internment camps. Many others, by word of mouth, learned of the safe haven in Le Chambon and made their way there. This band of brothers and sisters defied the evil that hovered over their nation as they instituted a sanctuary where people could be hidden away from the horror that was the Holocaust.

The angels who inhabited Le Chambon were supported with donations from the "Quakers, the Salvation Army, the American Congregational Church, the pacifist movement Fellowship of Reconciliation, Jewish and Christian ecumenical groups, the French Protestant student organization Cimade and the Swiss Help to Children . . . "140

With an amazing amount of organizational skill, people were found who agreed to house Jews—a deadly prospect for Jews and homeowners alike. The preparations for the influx of refugees were monumental—schools had to be organized for newly arrived children, false documents had to be provided, newcomers had to be trained in what to do if/when danger threatened, as did the inhabitants. It was a never-ending task to secure food for the newcomers as well as the farmers and their families on the outskirts of town.

Too many of the children that arrived in Le Chambon were orphans whose parents had been shipped to concentration camps in Germany, only to face certain death. The people of the Vivarais Plateau must certainly have agreed with Trocmé. When Vichy officials demanded a list of the Jews that resided in the area, Trocmé declined with,

"We do not know what a Jew is. We only know men."[141] While Trocmé urged the Jewish visitors to hold Shabbat services, they were also encouraged to attend meetings in his church in order to maintain the appearance of inclusion with the community.

It was inevitable that the humane actions of the people on the plateau would be noticed by some anti-Semitic members of Petain's government. Sure enough, the authorities roared into town one day and set forth to search for Jews in the area, many of them foreign-born and not French citizens. When the alarm was raised that Vichy or German security officials were nearby, the refugees were hidden further afield or taken by underground railroad to Switzerland.

The winter of 1942 brought shivers and goosebumps, but not just from the icy winds that blew in from the north. Germans arrived in Le Chambon. A French service organization, Service Francais des Relations Franco-Allemands, demanded 170 beds be made available for German military convalescents. The local Hotel du Lignon, situated on the main street of the town, was commandeered. Author Caroline Moorehead wrote in *Village of Secrets: Defying the Nazis in Vichy France*:

Soon the roads leading in and out of Le Chambon rang with the sounds of marching and singing. When the Chambonnais seemed to avoid them and disappeared as soon as they emerged, the Germans observed that it was obvious that the French had never cared for music . . . . For a while, the villagers with radios were terrified that they would be overheard listening to the French BBC service and reported. But as the Germans seemed intent on being friendly, behaving correctly, and doing what they could to avoid being returned to the eastern front, and as they expressed no interest of any kind in the foreigners and the refugees, the Chambonnais began to feel reassured . . . . Not least the oddest aspect of the plateau's war was the presence of all the German soldiers living in the very heart of the village, apparently unaware that they were surrounded on all sides by Jewish children.[142]

Most of the quests to protect the Jewish children of Le Chambon were successful, but one Nazi incursion brought great distress to the Trocmé family. Daniel, a second cousin and house director at one of the schools, was interrogated by the Gestapo during a raid. Rather than allow the Jewish students secreted in the school to be taken away alone, he determined to go with them. According to one of the young men arrested at the same time, Daniel had been questioned repeatedly during the journey to the internment camp at Majdanek in Poland. His fate was not learned until 1945 when the Russians captured the camp and discovered a ledger with the names and dates of those murdered there. It revealed that Daniel Trocmé was gassed and his body incinerated on April 4, 1944. Daniel was honored in 1976 as Righteous Among the Nations and a tree was planted at Yad Vashem in Jerusalem.

The clock had just struck 7:00 p.m. on the day before St. Valentine's Day 1943 when an ominous black vehicle pulled to a stop outside the home of André and Magda Trocmé. It was a rare sight, for there were few automobiles left since the Germans had occupied the area—and fewer still on their street. André was away from home, visiting those who housed refugees, when a knock sounded at the front door. Magda, aware of local customs, knew it was likely not a villager who would have simply opened the door and entered. Refugees seeking asylum would have arrived by train much earlier in the day. She approached the old, heavy door with trepidation and eased it open. Standing on the outside was the chief of police, Major Silvani, and one of his lieutenants. He, rather apologetically, demanded to know the whereabouts of her husband. The hour they had both anticipated and dreaded had arrived: Magda realized that André was about to be arrested, along with his associate, Edouard Theis, and their friend and local headmaster, Roger Darcissac.

Hallie recreated the scene of Trocmé's arrest:

> The three men [Silvani, his lieutenant and Trocmé] stepped out into the Rue de la Grande Fontaine.... The narrow, medieval street was dark, and [the wind] was blowing thin snow around the broken, ice-covered stones in the road. On both sides of the crooked street... villagers were lined up, looking fixedly at Trocmé as he walked between the two policemen.... As the three walked west down the street toward the high road that led to the village square, the bystanders began to sing the old Lutheran hymn "A Mighty Fortress Is Our God." A woman named Stekler, sister of a

half-Jew who had been arrested and released by the Vichy police, started the singing. The calm, deeply rooted song surrounded the three men, while the villagers closed behind them, and the *clop-clop* of their wooden shoes, muffled a little by the thin snow, followed them up the street.[143]

After having located and arrested Trocmé's other two cohorts, they were transported to Saint-Paul-d'Eyjeaux, an internment camp near Limoges. Their time there was well-spent, as Trocmé began to share the story of Le Chambon with the Communists interred in the facility. When asked why so many would risk their lives for Jews, the pastor was able to share the gospel with them. He began a religious service with twelve that quickly grew to forty over a few days. The men in his barracks soon learned the true meaning of compassion as the Chambonnais gathered gifts from their meager supplies for Magda and Darcissac's son to deliver to their pastor and father from their villagers.

After more than a month of confinement, the three men were summoned to the camp director's office. He offered them freedom if they would sign papers that promised their obedience of all orders given by Petain. In good conscience, Trocmé and Theis said they could not sign the document. Darcissac, a government employee, had already been required to sign the missive. The two men returned to their cellblock, expecting that they had just confirmed their death warrants.

The following morning, the two men were again called to the director's office and told unexpectedly that orders had come from top echelons ordering their release. They were forced to continue their work underground, but the rescue efforts continued unabated with the assistance of Magda and a plateau filled with friends and co-workers. In the early days of September 1944, the Vivarais Plateau and its inhabitants were liberated by the Free French 1st Armored Division.

Historian and author Terese Pencak Schwartz wrote:

> For every rescuer there were many anony-
> mous accomplices—people who helped, but who
> chose to remain anonymous. The anonymous
> accomplices would leave packages of food or
> supplies on a doorstep in the middle of the
> night. The anonymous accomplices would give
> a signal when a Nazi soldier approached. Many
> were accomplices just by remaining silent—by
> not saying anything, even when they knew

that their punishment could be torture or execution.[144]

It is rare that the State of Israel has recognized an entire area as Righteous Among the Nations, but in 1990 Le Chambon and towns of the Vivarais Plateau were so honored. That was followed in December 2007 by the awarding of forty individual designations as Righteous Among the Nations. Former French president Jacques Chirac visited Le Chambon on July 8, 2004, and recognized the bravery of its inhabitants. In January 2007, a ceremony in the Pantheon in Paris also honored the residents of Le Chambon.

André Trocmé was recognized as Righteous Among the Nations by Yad Vashem in January 1971, and Magda Trocmé in July 1986. Rev. Edouard Theis was granted a place on the Yad Vashem Wall of Honor on July 15, 1981.

The courage, heroism, and chivalry of the men, women, and children of Le Chambon and its neighboring towns during the Holocaust are unprecedented and exceptional. As evil closed in, they stood as beacons of light in the darkness of hatred and brutality.

ENDNOTES

1. "Michael Josephson quotes," *ThinkExist.com*, http://thinkexist.com/quotes/michael_josephson/; accessed October 2015.

2. "Hannah Senesh," *goodreads*, http://www.goodreads.com/author/show/98871.Hannah_Senesh; accessed October 2015.

3. Susan Brophy Down, *Irena Sendler: Bringing Life to Children of the Holocaust* (New York, NY: Crabtree Publishing, 2012), 55.

4. "Quotes About Light," *goodreads,* http://www.goodreads.com/quotes/tag/light; accessed November 2015.

5. George H. W. Bush's State of the Union Address, Envisioning One Thousand Points of Light, January 29, 1991, http://www.infoplease.com/ipa/A0900156.html; accessed August 2015.

6. "Hannah Senesh," *goodreads,,*http://www.goodreads.com/author/show/98871.Hannah_Senesh; accessed October 2011.

7. Miep Gies and Alison Leslie Gold, *Anne Frank Remembered: The Story of the Woman Who Helped to Hide the Frank Family* (New York: Simon and Schuster, 1987), 11.

8. Gies and Gold, 5.

9. Gies and Gold, 23.

10. Gies and Gold, 32.

11. Quoted by Thomas Weyr in *The Setting of the Pearl: Vienna Under Hitler* (New York: Oxford University Press, 2005), 27.

12. Joseph Koek, "A Hidden Child of the Holocaust Shares His Story at Augustana College," http://quadcityjournal.com/2013/04/08/a-former-hidden-child-of-the-holocaust-shares-his-story-at-augustana-college/; accessed September 2015.

13. Gies and Gold, 88.

14. Ibid.

15. Gies and Gold, 95–96.

16. "Anne and Fritz as Room Mates," http://www.annefrankguide.net/en-US/bronnenbank.asp?aid=26249; accessed September 2015.

17. Gies and Gold, 109.

18. Gies and Gold, 125.

19. Glenys Roberts, "Painfully shy, awesomely brave, the unknown heroine behind Anne Frank's diary," *Daily Mail.com* (13 January, 2010): http://www.dailymail.co.uk/news/article-1242725/Miep-Gies-Painfully-shy-awesomely-brave-unknown-heroine-Anne-Franks-diary.html#ixzz3phgdmWoB; accessed October 2015.

20. "Jan Gies Dies at 87; Helped Anne Frank Hide in Amsterdam," *New York Times* (January 28, 1993): http://www.nytimes.com/1993/01/28/world/jan-gies-dies-at-87-helped-anne-frank-hide-in-amsterdam.html; accessed October 2015.

21. "Omar Bradley," https://en.wikipedia.org/wiki/Omar_Bradley; accessed September 2015.

22. Gies and Gold, 196.

23. Gies and Gold, 196–197.

24. Gies and Gold, 204.

25. Gies and Gold, 231.

26. Gies and Gold, 246.

27. Jemma Saunders, "Who Betrayed Anne Frank?" http://www.historyinanhour. com/2014/08/04/betrayed-anne-frank/; accessed September 2015.

28. Gies and Gold, 263.

29. https://en.wikipedia.org/wiki/Netherlands_in_World_War_II; accessed August 2015.

30. Peter Longerich, *Holocaust: The Nazi Persecution and Murder of the Jews (New York, NY: Oxford University Press, 2010)*, 4.

31. Emilie Schindler with Erika Rosenberg, translated by Delores M. Koch, *Where Light and Shadow Meet: A Memoir* (New York, NY: W.W. Norton & Co., 1996), ix.

32. "Munich Agreement," https://en.wikipedia.org/wiki/Munich_Agreement; accessed October 2015.

33. David M. Crowe, *Oskar Schindler: The Untold Account of His Life, Wartime Activities, and the True Story Behind the List* (New York, NY: Basic Books, 2004), 66.

34. Crowe, 70–71.

35. "Poldek Pfefferberg," http://schindlerjews.com/page_11.htm; accessed October 2015.

36. Ibid.

37. *Longerich, 147.*

38. Longerich, 161.

39. Crowe, 179.

40. Crowe, 180.

41. Eric Silver, *The Book of the Just: The Unsung Heroes Who Rescued Jews from Hitler* (New York: Grove Press, 1992), 149.

42. Crowe, 185–186.

43. "Plaszow Concentration Camp in Krakow," Essential Krakow. Archived from the original on 4 September 2012; https://en.wikipedia.org/wiki/Krak%C3%B3w-P%C5%82asz%C3%B3w_concentration_camp; accessed October 2015.

44. Tadeusz Pankiewitz, *Apteka w Getcie Krakowskim* (Krakow: Wydawnictwo Parwnicze, 1956), 115. (Note: Pankiewitz was honored by Yad Vashem as Righteous Among the Nations for his efforts to save Jews, one of only a few non-Jewish Poles to survive the ghetto.)

45. Elinor J. Brecher, *Schindler's Legacy: True Stories of the List Survivors* (New York, NY: Penguin Group, 1994), 151.

46. "Rena Ferber," http://schindlerjews.com/page_8.htm; accessed October 2015.

47. Crowe, 388.

48. Crowe, 390.

49. "Testimony of Yitzhak Stern, Yitzhak Stern, May 1962, at a meeting of Schindler's survivors with their rescuer in Israel," Yad Vashem Archives, http://www.yadvashem. org/yv/en/righteous/stories/related/stern_testimony.asp; accessed October 2015.

50. "Schindler's Women," http://www.shoah.dk/Courage/Schindler.htm; accessed October 2015.

51. "Stella Müller-Madej," http://schindlerjews.com/page_13.htm; accessed October 2015.

52. "Emilie Schindler," http://www.oskarschindler.dk/schindler4.htm; accessed October 2015.

53. "Oskar Schindler," http://www.holocaustresearchproject.org/survivor/schindler. html; accessed October 2015.

54. Herbert Steinhouse, "The Real Oskar Schindler," April 1994, http://www.writing. upenn.edu/~afilreis/Holocaust/steinhouse.html; accessed October 2015.

55. "The Good German Schindler," *Daily Mail* (London), December 11, 1961, 8.

56. Dr. Moshe Bejski, "Notes on the Banquet in honor of Oskar Schindler," May 2, 1962, Tel Aviv, Israel, 16–17.

57. "Schindler's List," http://www.imdb.com/title/tt0108052/quotes; accessed May 2012.

58. Crowe, 627.

59. Down, 10.

60. Down, 19.

61. "Irena Sendler," May 22, 2008, *The Economist*, http://www.economist.com/node/11402658; accessed September 2015.

62. Down, 28.

63. "Kristallnacht (night of broken glass)," http://elginhistory12.wikispaces.com/Kristalln acht+%28+night+of+broken+glass%29; accessed September 2015.

64. Ibid.

65. Callum MacDonald, *The Killing of SS Obergruppenführer Reinhard Heydrich* (New York: The Free Press, 1989), 5.

66. "The Judenrat, or Jewish Council," http://www2.humboldt.edu/rescuers/book/Makuch/judrat.html; accessed November 2015.

67. Charles G. Roland, "Courage Under Siege: Starvation as Policy," http://remember.org/courage/chapter6; accessed September 2015.

68. Down, 48.

69. Jack Mayer, *Life in a Jar: The Irena Sendler Project* (Middlebury, VT: Long Trail Press, 2011), 155.

70. Down, 56.

71. Mayer, 165.

72. Jan Ciechanowski, *Defeat in Victory* (Garden City, NY: Doubleday, 1947), 182.

73. http://www.brainyquote.com/quotes/quotes/t/tseliot107488.html; accessed September 2015.

74. Transcript, "Eleanor Roosevelt," *American Experience* http://www.pbs.org/wgbh/americanexperience/features/transcript/eleanor-transcript/; accessed February 2012.

75. http://www.holocaustforgotten.com/karski2.htm; accessed November 2015.

76. "Irena Sendler," *Jewish Virtual Library*, http://www.jewishvirtuallibrary.org/jsource/biography/irenasendler.html; accessed July 2012; and Michael Bar-Zohar, *Beyond Hitler's Grasp: The Heroic Rescue of Bulgaria's Jews* (Avon, MA: Adams Media Corporation, 1998), 119.

77. Down, 91.

78. Mayer, 240.

79. "Poland 'co-responsible' for WWII says Russian ambassador," http://www.msn.com/en-us/news/world/poland-co-responsible-for-wwii-says-russian-ambassador/ar-AAeOuQL?li=AA54ur; accessed September 2015.

80. Ibid.

81. Ibid.

82. "Irena Sendler," *The Economist* (March 22, 2008): http://www.economist.com/node/11402658; accessed September 2015.

83. Mayer, 337.

84. Mayer, 345.

85. Stephen Keeler, "A Hidden Life: A Short Introduction to Chiune Sugihara," *Orthodoxy and the World* (May 20, 2008): http://www.pravmir.com/article_282.html; accessed October, 2015.

86. "Zionist Congress: Zionist Congresses during British Mandate," *Jewish Virtual Library,* http://www.jewishvirtuallibrary.org/jsource/Zionism/zionman.html; accessed September 2015.

87. "German-Soviet Boundary and Friendship Treaty," http://avalon.law.yale.edu/20th_century/gsbound.asp; accessed October 2015.

88. Hillel Levine, *In Search of Sugihara* (New York, NY: The Free Press, a Division of Simon & Shuster, Inc., 1996), 121.

89. Ibid, 135.

90. "Chiune Sugihara," *Jewish Virtual Library,* https://www.jewishvirtuallibrary.org/jsource/Holocaust/sugihara.html; accessed September 2015.

91. Quotation #39215 from Contributed Quotations," *The Quotations Page,* http://www.quotationspage.com/quote/39215.html; accessed September 2015.

92. Levine, 210.

93. Jaweed Kaleem, "Chiune Sugihara, Japan Diplomat Who Saved 6,000 Jews During Holocaust, Remembered," January 26, 2013, *Huffington Post,* http://www.huffingtonpost.com/2013/01/24/chiune-sugihara-japanese--jews-holocaust_n_2528666.html; accessed September 2015.

94. Levine, 252.

95. "Sugihara: An Interview with David Kranzler," http://www.pbs.org/wgbh/sugihara/readings/kranzler.html; accessed September 2015.

96. Marvin Tokayer and Mary Swartz, *The Fugu Plan: The Untold Story of the Japanese and the Jews During World War II* (Jerusalem, Israel: Paddington Press, Ltd., 1979; reprint, Jerusalem: Gefen Publishing House, 2004), 223.

97. Zamira Chenn, "Chiune Sugihara, The 'Japanese Schindler,'" *Jewish Post,* http://www.jewishpost.com/shalom/Chiune-Sugihara-The-Japanese-Schindler.html; accessed September 2015.

98. Corrie ten Boom, "Life is but a Weaving," http://www.goodreads.com/quotes/741391-life-is-but-a-weaving-the-tapestry-poem-my-life; accessed December 2015.

99. Corrie ten Boom, with John and Elizabeth Sherrill, *The Hiding Place* (Old Tappan, NJ: Spire Books, 1971), 58–59.

100. Ibid, 59.

101. Ibid, 61.

102. Ibid, 63.

103. Ibid, 101.

104. Ibid, 160.

105. Ibid, 196.

106. Msgr. John M. Oesterreicher, "Auschwitz, the Christian, and the Council," *Catholic Culture.org,* http://www.catholicculture.org/culture/library/view.cfm?recnum=609; accessed December 2015.

107. Corrie ten Boom, with John and Elizabeth Sherrill, *The Hiding Place,* 196.

108. Ibid, 212.

109. Ibid, 238.

110. "The Story of Raoul Wallenberg, College Life," *Wallenberg Legacy,* http://wallenberg.umich.edu/raoul-wallenberg/the-story-of-raoul-wallenberg/college-life/; accessed December 2015.

111. Kati Marton, *Wallenberg: The Incredible True Story of the Man Who Saved the Jews of Budapest* (New York, NY: Arcade Publishing, 2011), 22.

112. Ibid, 23.

113. John Bierman, *Righteous Gentile: The story of Raoul Wallenberg, missing hero of the Holocaust* (London: Penguin Books Ltd., 1981), 25.

114. "The Nuremberg Race Laws," http://www.ushmm.org/outreach/en/article. php?ModuleId=10007695; accessed December 2015.

115. Marton, 24.

116. Marton, 24–25.

117. "The 'Final Solution': The Wannsee Conference," *Jewish Virtual Library*; http://www. jewishvirtuallibrary.org/jsource/judaica/ejud_0002_0020_0_20606.html; accessed December 2015.

118. "While the Allies hold a conference in Bermuda, Jews in the Warsaw Ghetto wage a doomed battle against the Nazis," http://paperpen.com/heritage/350/look/look1.htm; accessed October 2015.

119. "Battle of Stalingrad," *History*, http://www.history.com/topics/world-war-ii/battle-of-stalingrad; accessed December 2015.

120. "War Refugee Board," *Holocaust Encyclopedia*, http://www.ushmm.org/wlc/en/ article.php?ModuleId=10007409; accessed January 2016.

121. "Documenting Wallenberg: A Compilation of Interviews with Survivors Rescued by Raoul Wallenberg," http://www.raoulwallenberg.net/wp-content/files_mf/135428465 9ebookdocumentingwallenberg.pdf; accessed January 2016.

122. Marton, 37.

123. David Metzler, "Raoul Wallenberg," *Jewish Virtual Library*, http://www. jewishvirtuallibrary.org/jsource/biography/wallenberg.html#lastditch; accessed January 2016.

124. Judy Mandelbaum, "Why did Raoul Wallenberg have to die?" *Judy's World* 18 January 2012, 2): http://judymandelbaum.com/articles.html;accessed August 2015.

125. "Raoul Wallenberg," *Rescuers*: http://auschwitz.dk/rescuers/id4.htm; accessed May 2015.

126. Ibid.

127. "A Swedish Rescuer in Budapest, Raoul Wallenberg," *Yad Vashem*, http://www. yadvashem.org/yv/en/righteous/stories/wallenberg.asp; accessed January 2016.

128. John Simkin, "Invasion of France," *Spartacus Educational* (September 1997, Updated August 2014): http://spartacus-educational.com/2WWfranceI.htm; accessed February 2016.

129. Paul Lee Tan, *Encyclopedia of 7,700 Illustrations: Signs of the Times* (Rockville, MD: Assurance Publishers, 1988), Item #55, 121.

130. "The Holocaust: The French Vichy Regime, The Statute on Jews," *Jewish Virtual Library*: http://www.jewishvirtuallibrary.org/jsource/Holocaust/VichyRegime.html; accessed February 2016.

131. Philip Hallie, *Lest Innocent Blood Be Shed* (New York, NY: HarperCollins, 1979), 41.

132. Ibid.

133. "Hitler, Petain Pledge Cooperation," *The Daily Chronicles of World War II*: http:// ww2days.com/hitler-petain-pledge-cooperation.html; accessed February 2016.

134. "Hitler Tours Paris, 1940," *EyeWitness to History*, http://www.eyewitnesstohistory. com/hitlerparis.htm; accessed February 2016.

135. Ibid.

136. "The Fuehrer Principle," *The History Learning Site*, *http*://www.historylearningsite. co.uk/nazi-germany/the-fuehrer-principle/; accessed February 2016.

137. Michael Curtis, "French Christian Decency and Hamas Evil," *American Thinker* (July 31, 2014): http://www.americanthinker.com/2014/07/french_christian_decency_and_ hamas_evil.html#ixzz3zDOGprbG; accessed February 2016.

138. Hallie, 135.

139. Robert M. Thomas Jr., "Magda Trocme, 94, Is Dead; Sheltered Victims of Nazis," *The New York Times* (October 19, 1996): http://www.nytimes.com/1996/10/19/world/ magda-trocme-94-is-dead-sheltered-victims-of-nazis.html; accessed October 2015.

140. "André and Magda Trocmé," *Wikipedia, https*://en.wikipedia.org/wiki/Andr%C3%A9_ and_Magda_Trocm%C3%A9; accessed February 2016.

141. Orna Raz, "We Do Not Know What A Jew Is. We Only Know Men," *The Times of Israel* (May 2, 2015): http://blogs.timesofisrael.com/we-do-not-know-what-a-jew-is-we- only-know-men/; accessed February 2016.

142. Caroline Moorehead, *Village of Secrets: Defying the Nazis in Vichy France* (New York, NY: Harper Collins, 2014), 166–167.

143. Hallie, 24.

144. Terese Pencak Schwartz, "Holocaust Rescuers: Heroes and Heroines of the Holocaust," *Holocaust Forgotten*, http://www.holocaustforgotten.com/rescuers.htm; accessed December 2015.

MICHAEL DAVID EVANS, the #1 *New York Times* bestselling author, is an award-winning journalist/Middle East analyst. Dr. Evans has appeared on hundreds of network television and radio shows including *Good Morning America, Crossfire* and *Nightline*, and *The Rush Limbaugh Show*, and on Fox Network, *CNN World News*, NBC, ABC, and CBS. His articles have been published in the *Wall Street Journal, USA Today, Washington Times, Jerusalem Post* and newspapers worldwide. More than twenty-five million copies of his books are in print, and he is the award-winning producer of nine documentaries based on his books.

Dr. Evans is considered one of the world's leading experts on Israel and the Middle East, and is one of the most sought-after speakers on that subject. He is the chairman of the board of the Ten Boom Holocaust Museum in Haarlem, Holland, and is the founder of Israel's first Christian museum—Friends of Zion: Heroes and History—in Jerusalem.

Dr. Evans has authored a number of books including: *History of Christian Zionism, Showdown with Nuclear Iran, Atomic Iran, The Next Move Beyond Iraq, The Final Move Beyond Iraq*, and *Countdown*. His body of work also includes the novels *Seven Days, GameChanger, The Samson Option, The Four Horsemen, The Locket, Born Again: 1967*, and *The Columbus Code*.

✦ ✦ ✦

Michael David Evans is available to speak or for interviews. Contact: EVENTS@drmichaeldevans.com.

BOOKS BY: MIKE EVANS

Israel: America's Key to Survival

Save Jerusalem

The Return

Jerusalem D.C.

Purity and Peace of Mind

Who Cries for the Hurting?

Living Fear Free

I Shall Not Want

Let My People Go

Jerusalem Betrayed

Seven Years of Shaking: A Vision

The Nuclear Bomb of Islam

Jerusalem Prophecies

Pray For Peace of Jerusalem

America's War:
The Beginning of the End

The Jerusalem Scroll

The Prayer of David

The Unanswered Prayers of Jesus

God Wrestling

The American Prophecies

Beyond Iraq: The Next Move

The Final Move beyond Iraq

Showdown with Nuclear Iran

Jimmy Carter: The Liberal Left
and World Chaos

Atomic Iran

Cursed

Betrayed

The Light

Corrie's Reflections & Meditations

The Revolution

The Final Generation

Seven Days

The Locket

GAMECHANGER SERIES:

GameChanger

Samson Option

The Four Horsemen

THE PROTOCOLS SERIES:

The Protocols

The Candidate

Persia: The Final Jihad

Jerusalem

The History of Christian Zionism

Countdown

Ten Boom: Betsie, Promise of God

Commanded Blessing

Born Again: 1948

Born Again: 1967

Presidents in Prophecy

Stand with Israel

Prayer, Power and Purpose

Turning Your Pain Into Gain

Christopher Columbus, Secret Jew

Living in the F.O.G.

Finding Favor with God

Finding Favor with Man

Unleashing God's Favor

The Jewish State: The Volunteers

See You in New York

Friends of Zion: Patterson & Wingate

The Columbus Code

The Temple

Satan, You Can't Have My Country!

Satan, You Can't Have Israel!

✓ Lights in the Darkness

COMING SOON:

Netanyahu

TO PURCHASE, CONTACT: orders@timeworthybooks.
com P. O. BOX 30000, PHOENIX, AZ 85046